STRANGE TALES

from

VIRGINIA'S FOOTHILLS

to the COAST

STRANGE TALES

from

VIRGINIA'S FOOTHILLS

to the COAST

THE RICHMOND VAMPIRE, THE WITCH
OF PUNGO, THE DISMAL SWAMP MONSTER
& MORE

DENVER MICHAELS

THE
History
PRESS

Published by The History Press
Charleston, SC
www.historypress.com

First published 2023

Manufactured in the United States

ISBN 9781467152716

Library of Congress Control Number: 2022948300

CONTENTS

Acknowledgements   7
Introduction   9

PART I. CRYPTIDS, MONSTERS AND OUT-OF-PLACE ANIMALS
1. The Virginia State Cryptid   17
2. The Mount Vernon Monster   23
3. Bigfoot   29
4. The Dismal Swamp Monster   38
5. Chessie   41
6. Other Weirdos   50
7. Urban Legends? Let's Hope So!   57

PART II. BURIED TREASURE
8. Colonial Gold   71
9. Pirate's Booty   80
10. Confederate Gold   89
11. The Government Wants the Gold   97

PART III. WEIRD STORIES
12. Mystery Booms   107
13. Ghost Lights and UFOs   114
14. The Witch of Pungo   121
15. Ghost Towns and Fake Towns   124

CONTENTS

16. A Good Conspiracy Is an Unprovable One   129
17. Old House Woods   143

Select Bibliography   149
About the Author   155

ACKNOWLEDGEMENTS

First things first, I have to thank my number-one fan, my lovely wife, Stefanie. Everyone should be so lucky to have a partner who believes in them the way she believes in me. Next, I want to thank my editor, Kate Jenkins; copyeditor Hilary Parrish; Crystal Murray; and all the other good folks at The History Press. I cannot express how thankful I am for the opportunities they have given me.

I need to give a shout-out to my buddy Jesse James Durdel, founder of the National Cryptid Society. I appreciate the strange reports he has shared with me over the years. Jesse is a talented artist, and I know readers will love his depiction of a devil monkey in the pages to follow.

Living in an RV and traveling full time presented some challenges to obtaining original photographs for this book, so I can't thank my daughter Nicole enough for her help. Also, the folks at Abandoned Country were kind enough to allow me to use one of their photographs. Make sure you check out their work and subscribe to their blog.

INTRODUCTION

A lot of good things start in Virginia; a lot of good things have started in Virginia. We're no strangers to firsts.
—Robert Hurt

The tan Ford Tempo in the Jamesway parking lot had a bumper sticker that read, "Virginia Is for Lovers." I was either eleven or twelve years old and had seen those stickers before. I asked my mother, "I see those stickers all the time; what are they supposed mean?"

"A lot of honeymooners come here," she replied.

"Why?" I asked.

"Well, there's a lot of things to do in Virginia."

"Yeah, right! Like what?"

"Well, you know, there's the beach. And there are places to go skiing, too. Virginia has a lot of history and stuff like that. Plus, it's really pretty here compared to a lot of states."

I didn't press the issue, but I wasn't buying what she was trying to sell me.

Like me, my wife was born and raised in the Old Dominion. I asked her one time what "Virginia Is for Lovers" meant. She didn't know, either. "That saying has been around forever, but I don't know what it's supposed to mean," she said.

I have posed the same question to friends and family—they do not know what the slogan means. Over the years, I have asked teachers, coworkers and professors at two community colleges where I took classes if they knew what

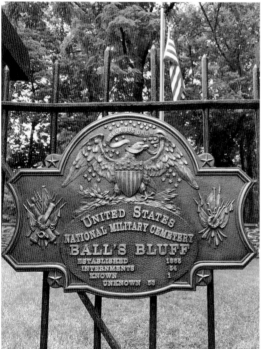

Above: Civil War history buffs enjoy visiting the Old Dominion's many battlefields. *Author's collection.*

Left: Ball's Bluff National Cemetery, north of Leesburg, holds the remains of fifty-four Union soldiers, fifty-three of whom are unknown, killed at the Battle of Ball's Bluff in 1861. *Author's collection.*

Countless old homes and hotels across Virginia, such as the Exchange Hotel in Gordonsville, served as hospitals during the Civil War. *Author's collection.*

One of the most unique Civil War memorials in Virginia is this marker for Confederate general Stonewall Jackson's amputated arm. The memorial lies off Route 20 near Locust Grove. *Author's collection.*

"Virginia Is for Lovers" meant. They were all as clueless as me.

I finally decided to read up on the catchy phrase. This is what I learned. The Commonwealth of Virginia has used the phrase "Virginia Is for Lovers" since 1969. It is the official tourism and travel slogan for the state. According to virginia.org, it is "one of the most beloved and iconic slogans in the world." The slogan entered the Madison Avenue Advertising Walk of Fame in 2019. It was also inducted into the Advertising Icon Museum. (I had no idea such accolades existed.) Forbes.com called "Virginia Is for Lovers" one of the top ten tourism marketing campaigns of all time.

"Virginia Is for Lovers" started out more specific and easier to understand. And don't tell her, but it looks like my mom might have been on the right track. According to virginia.org:

The phrase came from a creative team headed by George Woltz of Martin & Woltz Inc., the Richmond advertising agency that won the Virginia State Travel Service account in 1968. According to Martin, a $100-a-week copywriter named Robin McLaughlin came up with an advertising concept that read, "Virginia is for history lovers." For a beach-oriented ad, the headline would have read, "Virginia is for beach lovers"; for a mountains ad, "Virginia is for mountain lovers," and so on. Martin thought the approach might be too limiting. Woltz agreed, and the agency dropped the modifier and made it simply "Virginia is for Lovers." The new slogan debuted in a 1969 issue of Modern Bride.

So, there you have it. Virginia is for those who love mountains, the beach, history, wine and craft beer—you name it. Virginia.org even has a section devoted to hauntings and ghost tours and lists other "spooky ideas" on its website. With that in mind, I would like to think Virginia is for lovers of strange stories. Let's face it, the commonwealth is full of tales of buried treasure, undiscovered animals, mysterious lights in the sky, creepy urban

Above: This sign in the NASA Wallops Flight Facility Visitor Center pays tribute to space lovers. *Author's collection.*

Left: A marketing sign in Chincoteague with the "Virginia Is for Lovers" slogan. Chincoteague is a destination for both beach lovers and those who love wild horses. *Author's collection.*

legends and more. In the pages to follow, I will recount many of my favorite stories. I hope readers will come away with a greater appreciation for the Old Dominion. With devil monkeys, Bigfoot and werewolves lurking in the woods; a sea monster in the Chesapeake Bay; and pirate and Confederate gold in the ground, Virginia is full of mystery.

PART I

CRYPTIDS, MONSTERS AND OUT-OF-PLACE ANIMALS

Chapter 1

THE VIRGINIA STATE CRYPTID

Distinctions between North American apes, devil monkeys, hairy bipeds, and Bigfoot are nebulous and possibly arbitrary.
—George M. Eberhart,
Mysterious Creatures: A Guide to Cryptozoology

Sic Semper Tyrannis. Most every Virginian is familiar with the Latin phrase that serves as the commonwealth's motto. It appears on the state seal and the state flag. Contrary to what me and my buddies used to say when we were in school, the motto does not translate to "get your damn foot off my chest" but, rather, "thus always to tyrants." As an adult, I've come to think Virginia has a great flag and its motto is among the best in the nation. New Hampshire barely edges out Virginia with its motto: "live free or die."

Keeping with things Virginia, its state flower is the dogwood; the dogwood is also the state tree. The state bird is the cardinal. The commonwealth also has a state bat: the Virginia big-eared bat. The American foxhound is the official dog of Virginia. The Virginia state fish is divided into saltwater and freshwater categories, with the striped bass and brook trout taking the honors, respectively. Milk is Virginia's state drink, and George Washington's Rye Whiskey is the state spirit. The igneous rock Nelsonite serves as Virginia's state rock, and the eastern oyster is the state shell. Who knew there were so many official state things? My list is far from complete;

The Virginia state flag. *Wikimedia Commons.*

there are more state symbols than those I have mentioned. That said, in my mind a category is missing—the Commonwealth of Virginia does not have an official cryptid. I would like to change that.

If the president appointed me to the position of cryptid czar and I were in charge of assigning each state an official cryptid, I would designate Mothman as the West Virginia state cryptid. Obviously, the Jersey Devil would represent the Garden State. The Skunk Ape would take the coveted position in Florida. The Mogollon Monster is my pick for Arizona, and for Arkansas, I would choose the Ozark Howler. Both Vermont and New York could lay claim to Champ, the Lake Champlain monster. Champ is famous enough to represent two states. Though Virginia has its share of Chessie sightings, I would make Chessie the official cryptid of Maryland. Virginia, if I had my say, would claim the devil monkey as its state cryptid.

According to eyewitnesses, devil monkeys have dark hair with white hair on their necks and bellies. Most have a doglike snout, pointed ears and long teeth and claws. Witnesses claim devil monkeys look like lemurs. But then, other observers say they resemble baboons. There are also reports that the creatures look like dogs from a distance. Obviously, devil monkey descriptions vary. For instance, sometimes they are about three feet long, but in other encounters, they reach eight feet. Some have tails; some do not. Author and researcher Mark A. Hall coined the term *devil monkey*, but there is no consensus within the cryptozoology community as to what devil monkeys are.

Folks have spotted devil monkeys all across the nation, but I think the best reports come from Virginia. Weird scenes unfolded in Smyth County in 1959, when a devil monkey started jumping on cars. A demented devil monkey leaped onto a convertible car and tore the top off with a driver and passenger inside. Thankfully, no one was hurt in the attack. Presumably, the same devil monkey latched onto a moving automobile and pressed its

A depiction of a fierce devil monkey. *Courtesy of Jesse James Durdel.*

face against the passenger window and for a time kept up with the car. Understandably, the creature gave those inside quite a scare. No one was injured in the encounter, but the disturbed primate left deep scratches along the entire length of the car. Fourteen years later, a man driving between Marion and Tazewell with his windows down had a devil monkey burst from the woods, run up to his car and take a swing at his arm.

In 2010, Goochland County became a devil monkey hot spot. Rumors of a strange creature matching devil monkey descriptions spread through the area in December. The *Goochland On My Mind* blog ran a couple of posts on area sightings. According to the blog, the creature was not an animal known to reside in Goochland County. It was not a deer or coyote, and "stable, sober folks" described the creature as being larger than a deer with a long, furry tail, long nose and pointed ears. The mystery animal stood on four legs, and its front legs were shorter than its rear legs. The creature displayed "menacing behavior" and showed its teeth to eyewitnesses before bounding away in "long, powerful strides."

Rumors of the devil monkey roaming Goochland County prompted Emily Neal to start a blog dedicated to sightings of the creature. In one of her posts, she included a list of people who had spotted the devil monkey. A fellow named Henry spotted it on November 17; Tom saw it near the high school on November 26; on December 1, Tommy say the creature near the fairgrounds; Jerry spotted it on Riddles Bridge Road on December 4; and Cheryl had a sighting at Goochland Courthouse on December 7.

Neal also included an unsubstantiated report in which a "lady in Food Lion" saw the creature outside her home on December 4 or 5. The lady noted that the mysterious animal scared her dogs. In another blog post, Neal mentioned that on the week ending on December 5, "some sort of creature, unknown to me what but reported to be a devil monkey, blocked traffic in Oilville."

Richmond station NBC 12 took an interest in Goochland's devil monkey sightings and ran an article on its website. NBC 12 contacted the sheriff's office and learned local police were not taking the matter seriously. Police believed the devil monkey sightings were a hoax, "the implication being that people in Goochland are seeing things due to the cold weather and long nights."

The article pointed to a loose spider monkey being the possible culprit behind the sightings, a suggestion that did not sit well with Emily Neal. Neal wrote, "Where on Earth did she get spider monkey from? It is a small, 25 pound monkey from Central and South America." Neal noted that devil monkeys are "tall and also kind of resemble a kangaroo, according to eyewitnesses." She went on, "No matter what the Goochland Devil Monkey turns out to be, they are not the same creature. I guarantee that to you."

Reacting to the NBC 12 piece, S.E. Warwick, writing on the *Goochland On My Mind* blog, took a wait-and-see approach to the spate of sightings and said, "Let's see what sort of evidence may appear in the coming weeks before declaring these episodes a hoax." She noted the people who had come forward with sightings were reliable and did not have a reason to fake their claims. In a brilliant, sharp rebuke of those who would scoff at the devil monkey sightings, Warwick wrote, "Using ridicule to suppress information outside the realm of 'normal' is a subtle yet effective form of mind control designed to discourage questioning of the status quo."

What was on the loose in Goochland County? And what is a devil monkey? These are not easy questions to answer. In some cases, an escaped exotic pet or zoo animal might be behind the sightings. A baboon or lemur on the run in an unfamiliar environment would surely possess the potential for aggression typical of devil monkey reports.

In other cases, due to their kangaroo-like appearance, devil monkeys might actually be out-of-place kangaroos or wallabies. There is a lot of overlap in so-called errant kangaroo sightings and devil monkey reports. That might be for a good reason. At least in some instances, these "phantom" kangaroos and psycho monkeys might be one and the same. Cryptozoologists Loren Coleman and Patrick Huyghe suggested that devil monkeys, which appear to leap, are sometimes mistaken for kangaroos. According to Coleman and Huyghe, due to the size and method of movement of devil monkeys, "they have evolved a large flat foot with three rounded toes. Immature Devil Monkeys resemble marsupials such as wallabies due to convergent evolution but this similarity diminishes as they mature."

Some have proposed that out-of-place coatis, also known as coatimundis, are mistaken for devil monkeys—at least in cases where the devil monkey's size is on the small end of the spectrum. Coatis are native to South America, Central America, Mexico and parts of the American Southwest. Coatis are dark in color and have elongated snouts and long tails with light underbellies.

Writing to the editor of the *Goochland Gazette*, Goochland County resident Donovan Paul Yates discussed his 2010 devil monkey sighting. The animal was too far away to see in detail, but it "appeared to walk in an ape-like manner." On June 25, 2014, Yates saw the strange creature again, and this time, he got a good look at it. It "walked mostly on its hind feet with balance touches occasionally with the front legs." The creature's coat was dark, and

A drawing of a coati from the University of Amsterdam's Iconographia Zoologica collection. *Wikimedia Commons.*

it had an elongated, tapered snout and a long tail. Said Yates, "I have seen this species of animal before. It is a South American Coatimundi."

Does an escaped coati explain away the Goochland devil monkey? Maybe, though reports indicated the creature in question was larger than a deer—not a good fit for a coati. If witnesses misjudged the size of the creature, then the coati explanation might be in play, and coatis might explain other devil monkey incidents, too. However, in my opinion, coatis are not a good explanation for the devil monkey phenomenon as a whole. So, what is a good explanation for devil monkeys? This is hard to say, and I don't take a strong stance on the issue. But I will say if Bigfoot is lurking in the woods, as many believe, why not another, smaller primate?

Chapter 2

THE MOUNT VERNON MONSTER

I believe in true love. But my opinion is tainted, because I also believe in Bigfoot,
aliens, and in the existence of honest politicians.
—*Jarod Kintz*

If you grew up in Virginia, then you know the commonwealth touts itself as the "mother of presidents." No other state in the Union has produced more presidents than the Old Dominion. When we were kids, teachers and administrators pounded that piece of trivia into our heads at school. My mom even brought it up once after I grumbled that Virginia was boring—as if somehow Zachary Taylor being born in Barboursville made Virginia livelier than the Big Apple, more hip than Southern California and as fun as the sun-kissed beaches of Florida.

Aside from the aforementioned Taylor, who died sixteen months into his first term, seven other Virginians have occupied the highest office in the land. They are George Washington, Thomas Jefferson, James Madison, James Monroe, William Henry Harrison, John Tyler and Woodrow Wilson.

There is a lot of weirdness associated with the presidents. For instance, Thomas Jefferson believed mammoths and mastodons were alive during his day and occupied the wild, unexplored lands in the West. I think Jefferson may have been right, but that is a subject for another time. President Lincoln hinted that an ancient race of giants inhabited America—a belief frowned upon today. Many ghost stories are associated with Lincoln; Honest Abe has been haunting the White House since his assassination. Though Lincoln is

Above: Zachary Taylor, the twelfth president of the United States, was born at Montebello in Orange County in 1784. *Courtesy of Nicole Pierce.*

Opposite, top: The birthplace of George Washington in Westmoreland County is a national monument. *Author's collection.*

Opposite, bottom: James Monroe was born in Westmoreland County in 1758. *Author's collection.*

"A view of Mount Vernon with the Washington family on the terrace," by Benjamin Henry Latrobe (1796). *Wikimedia Commons.*

the most talked about White House ghost, other presidents still linger there, too. Many have heard the laugh of "Old Hickory," Andrew Jackson. John Tyler haunts the Blue Room, and William Henry Harrison lurks in the attic. As you might imagine, many of the historic homes where the presidents lived also claim hauntings today. With these things in mind, it is only fitting that a wooded area near George Washington's Mount Vernon estate had a monster on the loose during the late 1970s and early 1980s.

In 1978, Mount Vernon area residents began hearing awful screams coming from the woods at night. No one knew what was making the frightening cries. The *Washington Post* described the commotion as a "muted wail—like someone being strangled in the shower." The same article said witnesses "described the sound as something like a wild boar, really loud frogs, some guy blowing in a wine bottle, a barred (or hoot) owl, a broken microphone on a CB outfit, a parrot, a mouse with an amplifier, a strangled dog, the ghost of George Washington and the ghost of George Washington's pigs." One witness, who was eleven years old when he first heard the screams, said the creature was most active between midnight and 5:00 a.m. He recalled, "People said it would cause their windows to rattle. We could hear it through our storm windows."

Residents were so alarmed by the odd nocturnal screams that the Fairfax County Police Department became involved. In May 1979, they commissioned a helicopter from the U.S. Park Police equipped with infrared cameras to search the area. The helicopter scanned a one-hundred-acre wooded lot where the screams had been taking place. Six police officers with radios positioned themselves at various points on the property while the helicopter hovered overhead. But the high-tech search did not find anything.

Dr. William Hark, who lived nearby, said, "I suspect it frustrates the police because they have not been able to catch it."

According to the *Washington Post*, Thelma Crisp, who lived on Union Farm Road at the time, told neighbors she had seen "a creature in her backyard that stands six feet tall and walks upright." Unfortunately, local police discouraged her from talking about her experiences. It is interesting to note that Michael Berger, a PhD employed by the National Wildlife Federation, thought the strange screams did not sound human. Berger said, "It's hard to describe, ah, it is a series of screams, not really screams, more like wails. They seemed to be fairly close to Thelma's house."

By the early 1980s, reports of the eerie screams had waned. To this day, the identity of the creature remains a mystery. Many think the Mount Vernon Monster was a Bigfoot. This might be the case. After all, Thelma Crisp saw something tall walking upright in her backyard.

I used to work with a fellow who grew up in Mount Vernon. He told me once about hearing the eerie screams of the Mount Vernon Monster as a kid. I lost contact with him years ago, but I remember him saying, "Man, that thing was scary and loud."

"What do you think it was?" I asked him.

"Beats me. But I know for a fact it wasn't a bobcat or fox."

"Well, what does that leave, then?"

"No idea. Some people say it was Bigfoot. But I don't believe in that crap."

His brother was more open to the idea of Bigfoot. He told me, "I don't know what it was. Call me crazy, but it sounded just liked the supposed Bigfoot audio recordings on shows like *MonsterQuest*."

The idea of the Mount Vernon Monster being a Bigfoot brings to mind another report from the early 1980s in Fairfax County. Several people claimed to see a "green-eyed Bigfoot" near McLean. The now-defunct website Cryptozoology News ran a story about the encounter in 2016. Predictably, a lot of locals laughed at the story. Think about it—a Bigfoot sighting in urbanized McLean sounds ridiculous. But in the early 1980s, Fairfax County was much different than it is today. According to the U.S. census, in 1980 there were 596,901 residents in Fairfax County, while in 2020, the number had swollen to 1,150,309. With the expansion of roads, addition of Metrorail lines and runaway housing and commercial development, most of Fairfax County is unrecognizable from what it was in the 1980s. So maybe Bigfoot was lurking in Fairfax County forty years ago.

I have experienced the rapid development of Northern Virginia firsthand. An economic downturn in the early 1980s forced my family to leave southwestern Virginia when I was in middle school. We relocated to Loudoun County, largely rural at the time. Today, the backroads, woods and farms outside Sterling, Ashburn and Leesburg are long gone. McMansions, subdivisions full of single-family homes and row upon row of townhouses stand in their place. An almost continuous strip mall runs from the Fairfax County line all the way past Leesburg. Sometimes I wonder if the powerful land developers and their lobbyists have pushed out Bigfoot. What stories will Loudoun, Stafford, Fauquier, Culpeper and Spotsylvania Counties tell decades from now? Surely the tales will make us pine for the old days when there was enough undeveloped land to support Bigfoot.

But then again, maybe all is not lost in the sea of Northern Virginia urban sprawl. In 2011, a Woodbridge resident called the police and said he saw "a coyote, or a werewolf" in the woods near his home. A werewolf in Woodbridge? Maybe things are all right after all.

Chapter 3

BIGFOOT

Bigfoot may well be an extraterrestrial, because…remember Chewbacca?
—*George Noory*

The ASA Monster

What if I told you the United States Marine Corps—the finest fighting force in the world—has a Bigfoot lurking on one of its bases? It's true. The legendary beast has made a home for itself on Marine Corps Base Quantico (MCBQ), and from the looks of things, the marines cannot do a thing about it. As early as 1957, a marine stationed at Quantico had an encounter with the beast, and he shared his story with the Bigfoot Field Researchers Organization (BFRO) in 2000. In report number 679, he wrote:

> *I observed something that looked like a bear while walking my post. What alerted me was a dog that use to walk post with whoever was on duty at night. When she started to bark I looked up and saw a figure that was about 7 feet tall* [and] *had light brownish hair on its body.* [I] *was not able to see the face due to the darkness of the wooded area, but when I told the dog to go after it, the figure just stayed there and didn't move, but when I put a round in the chamber of my M1 it took off running.*

In the late 1970s, there were so many Bigfoot sightings on MCBQ that area newspapers took an interest in the creature. The *Sunday Times* in

Salisbury, Maryland, ran a story on February 6, 1977, titled "Marines May Have 'Big Foot' of Their Own." The piece began by stating that marines on guard duty had been hearing strange sounds at night. The creature had been frequenting an ammunition storage area, and marines dubbed it the "ASA Monster." According to the article:

> *A few Marines claim to have seen "brown things" walking on two legs. Others say they have heard strange shrieking screams, and some claim they've heard something climbing a fence.*
>
> *"I remember the night I saw it very well," said a Marine who asked that his name not be used. "It was about 2 a.m., I was walking my post when I heard something in the woods. I stopped and looked in the direction of the noise. I could see a dark figure beyond the fence just in front of the tree line, so I shined my flashlight at it. I couldn't believe what I saw. It was some kind of creature that looked like a cross between an ape and a bear. The first thing I noticed was its large glaring eyes. Then I noticed it had arms and was covered with dark brown hair."*

The marine, who (for good reason) wished to remain anonymous, said the creature stood between six and eight feet in height and resembled drawings he had seen of Bigfoot.

The *Potomac News* ran a piece on the ASA Monster on January 17, 1977. According to the article, authorities at the base had ordered marines to keep their mouths shut about the monster:

> *We called the ASA (Ammunition Storage Area) sergeant of the guard to determine whether there had been any more sightings or sounds in the area but were told that all information regarding the "ASA Monster" is considered "classified." When asked why that is so, the guard answered that he was not allowed to answer that question either.*
>
> *He later said that the information is not really "classified" but everyone at the compound has been ordered not to talk about the monster at all.*

A marine came forward in 2021 and reported his MCBQ Bigfoot sighting to the BFRO. The 1994 encounter occurred near Camp Upshur. He and his squad were on a training mission when they spotted something strange. Report number 71904 states:

According to this display at the International Cryptozoology Museum in Portland, Maine, this is what Bigfoot scat should look like. *Author's collection.*

With my night vision I saw what looked to be something estimated 8 feet high. I could see shoulders of something on both sides of this huge oak tree. We were startled. No civilian was allowed in this restricted area. We hastily crossed [the] road [and] met [the] other 2 platoons on other side of road. [We] gave our security password and proceeded on the mission.

When we returned to base, we reported the incident to the commanding officer. He replied, "It's a restricted area. That's impossible." Nothing was spoken of it again.

MCBQ is an enormous base, much of which is heavily wooded. The base spans more than fifty-five thousand acres, or eighty-six square miles. The forests on MCBQ are full of deer, coyotes, turkey, bear and other game animals. MCBQ allows hunting during Virginia's hunting season, but much of the base is off-limits even during this time. Moreover, the sixteen-thousand-acre Prince William Forest Park is adjacent to the base. The National Park Service manages Prince William Forest Park, the largest area of protected land in the Washington, D.C. metropolitan area. A number of Bigfoot sightings have occurred here. Having visited the park many times, I think it is the kind of place Bigfoot could thrive—and hide. I think it is possible that between MCBQ and Prince William Forest Park there could be a Bigfoot population lurking in the shadows.

Follow the Water

"Follow the water" is a common phrase that Bigfoot researchers, authors, YouTubers, hobbyists and enthusiasts proclaim on social media. They believe following creeks and rivers and staking out lakes, ponds and swamps is a surefire way to get close to the elusive beast. Maybe they are right. What I believe is still the best video evidence for the existence of Bigfoot, the 1967 Patterson-Gimlin film, shot in Northern California, shows a Bigfoot walking along Bluff Creek, a tributary of the Klamath River. So-called experts have debated the authenticity of the film for decades. Some think it shows a Bigfoot, while others say it is a man in a suit. Regardless of what it shows—a huckster in a costume or a Bigfoot—fifty-five years later, the Patterson-Gimlin film remains the gold standard for Bigfoot video footage.

In 2014, Randy O'Neal photographed an alleged Bigfoot along the shore of the Intracoastal Waterway in Virginia. O'Neal's Bigfoot pictures were not the typical blurry photos so often associated with the creature.

They were clear and showed what looked to be a dark-colored bipedal creature. "Finally, a photo that is not blurry nor hidden behind a tree. A clear photo of Bigfoot standing out in the wide open. You be the judge," said O'Neal.

O'Neal posted the photographs to his YouTube channel and told the story of an encounter he had in the same spot about twenty-five years earlier. He wrote, "My dad, a friend of ours and myself had a late night run-in with an unknown creature." The trio were camping and had been fishing and "shooting beer cans." After they settled in for the evening, O'Neal saw a set of red eyes peering at the group from behind the bushes. O'Neal, fifteen years old at the time, was frightened, and his father handed him a shotgun and told him to shoot the red-eyed stalker. O'Neal fired in the direction of the beast, and it "let out the most blood curdling scream." It went running through the woods and into the water. When it hit the water, it "sounded like a Volkswagen" had made the splash. The following morning, the trio discovered the creature had cleared a path on its way to the water "as if a skid steer had gone through the woods"; it did not leave a sapling standing.

Is Bigfoot lurking in the forests around Lake Anna? According to eyewitness reports, the answer is yes. *Author's collection.*

Long before O'Neal snapped a picture of a Bigfoot that had followed the water, all the way back in 1981, the *Washington Post* reported that a Bigfoot was frequenting Northwest River Park in Chesapeake. The creature had earned the nickname "Skunkfoot" due to its awful smell. Witness descriptions of a terrible odor are common in Bigfoot reports. For instance, a lady from Florida contacted me through my website and told me of her Bigfoot encounter in a wilderness preserve in Pasco County. She said, "I could smell it. It was horrendous…my God the smell of it."

I have heard of Bigfoot sightings along the Shenandoah, James and New Rivers. Most stories have come from kayakers and canoers who have had encounters while lazily floating along. Recently, the website Phantoms and Monsters told of a Bigfoot encounter in Mecklenburg County along the Meherrin River. There has also been a slew of Bigfoot sightings over the years from Spotsylvania and Louisa Counties near Lake Anna.

It seems as if the "follow the water" crowd is on to something. But really, there is nothing revolutionary about looking for Bigfoot along waterways. All animals can be found near water because they need water to survive. Animals have to make regular trips to a water source. Predators know this and stake out watering holes. Think of how many nature films you have

Opposite: A white-tailed deer crossing a creek in Glacier National Park. For obvious reasons, game animals are attracted to water. *Author's collection.*

Above: An abundance of tracks next to a stream in southern Virginia. *Author's collection.*

Right: An eighteenth-century dowser searching for water. *Wikimedia Commons.*

Rain or shine, hot or cold—streams such as this in central Virginia are a smart place to look for Bigfoot. *Author's collection.*

seen in which lions ambush poor unsuspecting wildebeests as they go for a drink of water. Even brackish water and salt water are good places to look for Bigfoot because of the food sources they provide. Presumably, Bigfoot collects clams, mussels and oysters; catches fish; and kills waterfowl in brackish water and salt water.

Water sources are excellent travel routes for both animals and humans. Naturally, one might expect to encounter a Bigfoot near water traveling, hunting, gathering or just getting a drink. But in my mind, where water comes into play the most is in finding tracks. Footprints are easier to make out in the damp soil along riverbanks and lake shores than they are in the woods.

But what if—as some believe—Bigfoot is not a physical creature unknown to science but something more akin to a ghost? Again, we have good news— follow the water. Many paranormal investigators think water acts as a conduit for the supernatural. Look no further than dowsing, a form of divination once widely used to locate sources of groundwater. Many cultures have tales of water spirits such as nymphs, water horses and mermaids and mermen.

Some think water "records" energy signatures, and this could presumably "play back" in the form of strange activity or the appearance of mysterious creatures. So again, follow the water if you're looking for Bigfoot—even if you do not think of Bigfoot as a physical being.

Who knows, maybe someday a person out looking for the ever-elusive Bigfoot might find some sort of indisputable evidence for its existence in Virginia—probably along a river.

Chapter 4

THE DISMAL SWAMP MONSTER

I'm the product of six million years of evolution?
Come on, man. I crawled out of a swamp yesterday.
—Peter Steele

A strange, vicious monster was on the loose in the Great Dismal Swamp around the turn of the twentieth century. The creature was "larger than a wolf, with shaggy, yellow hair," and it killed livestock and dogs and even attacked area residents. Communities bordering the Great Dismal Swamp were on edge, and the monster "made people afraid to leave their homes at night." Armed residents formed search parties to go after the monster, but it eluded them. That is, until Harrison Walker, a local hunter, "unexpectedly killed" the creature.

Shortly after Harrison Walker killed the monster, it—or another of its ilk—struck again. Edward Smith, a local farmer, claimed that "a strange being visited his premises and killed seven dogs, two of which were eaten outright." The intruder mutilated the bodies of five of Smith's dogs. One dog escaped the monster's clutches and hid underneath a barn; it alerted Smith with its incessant barking. According to an article that appeared in the *Daily Morning Journal and Courier*, a New Haven, Connecticut newspaper, once Smith heard the dog, he ran out with a pistol in his hand. Smith described the animal as "larger than a wolf, with shaggy yellow hair, long head and sunken eyes." According to the paper, "The monster sprang upon him. In getting away Smith fell and the beast sprang upon his body, tearing his clothes to shreds. He finally beat it off. The revolver, being corroded, would not fire."

The Dismal Swamp Monster continued its harassment of area residents. The *Richmond Dispatch* reported the following on February 18, 1902:

> *L. Frank Ames, a merchant at Benet's Creek, thirteen miles from Suffolk, on Thursday night had an experience with the Dismal Swamp monster, which earlier this week killed seven of Edward Smith's dogs, ate two of them, and attacked Smith himself. Ames said he shot at the strange animal several times without effect. Six of his dogs were sent after it, but they fled in terror and hid. The monster escaped....Superstitious persons are much upset over the strange visits, and farmers are fearing for the safety of their stock. The thing is described as of long, gaunt form, vicious eyes, and shaggy, yellow hair.*

The creature's reign of terror continued as it killed and ate dogs, livestock and small animals. The monster, "whose eyes at night shone with a phosphorescent glow," spawned stories that caused many locals to avoid going out at night. But finally, on April 12, 1902, the Dismal Swamp Monster met its end. The *Richmond Times* reported:

> *The animal was shot dead by a huntsman while it was in the act of devouring a dog just killed. The description is similar to that given of the beast beforehand. It looks more like a wolf than anything else. Crowds of people went to the scene and inspected the monster, whose body was left near the station where it died.*

The story of the Dismal Swamp Monster faded away after the second strange animal was killed. News stories after this only recapped prior events. It should not come as a surprise that today, the 1902 tales of a large, wolf-like creature have morphed into stories of a seven-foot dogman and/or Bigfoot on many internet sites. And while I believe most anything could be hiding in the Great Dismal Swamp, up to and including a Bigfoot and a dogman, the aforementioned newspaper articles make it clear this is not what was terrorizing local residents.

What was the creature that spread havoc throughout the Great Dismal Swamp communities? Was it a wolf? An exotic animal? Maybe something that escaped a zoo, traveling circus or private collection? During the height of the Dismal Swamp Monster saga, the *Richmond Dispatch* asked if the creature on the loose could be another "Hanover lion." According to the paper, ten to fifteen years prior to the Dismal Swamp Monster sightings, residents "were

Folks cannot get enough of Bigfoot. From internet stories where it does not belong to quaint campgrounds in Virginia, the elusive beast is popping up everywhere. *Author's collection.*

in a tumult of excitement and dread" in Henrico and Hanover Counties after a "lion or tiger had escaped from a menagerie." Locals tracked down and killed the Hanover lion. But examination of its body revealed it was not a lion or a tiger at all. Instead, it was "a huge mastiff, a dog not as common in these parts then as now." Sadly, the mastiff belonged to a "foreign gentleman" visiting the area who had been searching for his beloved dog when locals shot it to death. Understandably, he was outraged that those who killed his canine friend "did not know how to distinguish between a lion and a dog."

The Hanover lion story makes me wonder if the Dismal Swamp Monster might have been a large breed of dog unfamiliar to the locals. Unfortunately, we will never know. We will probably never know what else is lurking in the impenetrable, soggy thickets of the Great Dismal Swamp, either.

Chapter 5

CHESSIE

Men really need sea-monsters in their personal oceans. An ocean without its
unnamed monsters would be like a completely dreamless sleep.
—John Steinbeck, The Log from the Sea of Cortez

The Chesapeake Bay is the largest estuary (a body of water where salt water and fresh water mix) in the United States and third largest in the world. The bay and its tidal tributaries have a whopping 11,684 miles of shoreline and a surface area of 4,480 miles. These waters hold more than 3,700 plants and animals. The Chesapeake produces half a billion pounds of seafood per year. Though seafood is king in the Chesapeake Bay, it is known for more than oysters, blue crabs and striped bass. According to legend, a sea monster is lurking in its waters.

Eyewitnesses claim the Chesapeake Bay monster resembles a giant serpent. Size estimates place the creature between twenty and forty feet in length. Most say it is about as big around as a telephone pole. Some claim the monster has a set of flippers, while others say it has a featureless body. When swimming, the creature holds its head steady about three feet above the water. It moves its body with horizontal undulations, similar to a snake, or with vertical undulations. The vertical movements give it a "multi-humped" appearance, common in sea serpent and lake monster reports all over the world.

Although it was dubbed "Chessie" by a *Richmond Times-Dispatch* reporter in 1977, sightings of the Chesapeake Bay monster date back to the nineteenth century. In 1840, workers aboard two schooners near present-day North Point State Park in Maryland spotted a creature in the water about twelve feet in length with four fins. Oddly, the witnesses claimed a shell covered the creature's body. In 1846, Captain Lawson saw an animal with a small head and sharp protrusions jutting from its back off the coast of Virginia. Lawson's ship was between Cape Henry on the mainland and Cape Charles on the Virginia peninsula when he spotted the creature.

Chessie made sporadic visits to the Chesapeake and its tributaries from the 1930s through the 1960s. However, Chessie's heyday was in the late 1970s and early 1980s. There were so many sightings of Chessie during this time frame that it became a household name around the bay and attracted attention from news outlets nationwide. In 1978, by the month of June, about thirty people had spotted a "long, ugly creature" in the bay.

In June 1980, Godwin Muse, a farmer from Westmoreland County, Virginia, saw a "fourteen-foot snake" in the Potomac River. Less than two weeks later, G.F. Green, his family and a friend spotted Chessie about fifteen miles downstream from the Muse sighting. The animal they saw had several

Is there a sea monster swimming in the depths of the Chesapeake Bay? *Author's collection.*

The East River in Mathews County. *Author's collection.*

humps and was twenty-five feet long and six inches in diameter. The creature was a fast swimmer and moved with "fluid motions."

Virginia Beach resident Bob White Sr. spotted "a large, strange and awesome thing that was certainly no manatee" near the Bay Bridge Tunnel. The snakelike creature held its head about four feet above the water. White passed over the animal in his boat. It was between fifteen and twenty feet long on the starboard side and over ten feet long on the port side.

In March 1985, Bill Reese spotted Chessie in the East River near his home in Mathews County, Virginia. The creature "swam with vertical humps" and was about a foot in diameter, twenty feet long and greenish-brown in color. In May, Reese spotted a similar creature, though smaller, that swam "horizontally like a snake" rather than vertically.

The most compelling Chessie account occurred in Maryland waters on May 31, 1982. Robert and Karen Frew had guests over for Memorial Day at their Kent Island home. The Frews and their guests noticed something large and snakelike moving in the bay. Robert Frew watched the creature through a pair of binoculars for a couple of minutes and then grabbed his video camera and captured several minutes of film. Frew's film showed a thirty-foot snakelike creature, but it was not of sufficient quality to

The author kayaking in the Chesapeake Bay and wondering if Chessie is out there. *Author's collection.*

positively identify the animal in question. After viewing the tape himself, Mike Frizzell of the Enigma Project, a paranormal research group active during the 1980s, reached out to the Smithsonian Institute and requested it study the tape. Smithsonian scientists agreed to view the tape and were intrigued when they watched it. However, due to the quality of the video, they failed to reach any conclusions. The tape then made its way to the Johns Hopkins Applied Physics Laboratory, where it was graphically enhanced. Unfortunately, funding for the project dried up, and work on the tape ceased. The enhancement did prove, however, that the tape showed a living animal rather than an inanimate object.

As recently as 2014, Chessie made an appearance in the Magothy River in Anne Arundel County, Maryland. Chris Gardner saw a "long, snakelike creature slithering through the water with a serpentine motion." The creature was over twenty feet long and black in color. According to Gardner, "It did not rise completely out of the water; however, its head and tail (or close to the tail) breached the surface with the rest of the body in between just submerged." Gardner recalled he first believed he saw two animals swimming in a straight line. However, he was able to rule out the possibility and said, "The water flow it created as it slithered along at a slow-walking pace told me it was one continuous creature. The water disturbance was an unbroken and continuous form." Gardner watched the creature for over a minute before it disappeared.

WHAT IS CHESSIE?

Explanations for Chessie run the gamut. Depending on who you ask or what you believe, Chessie could be anything such as a prehistoric holdover, an enormous snake, a manatee or even logs floating in the water. Chessie's serpentine appearance has led some to believe the creature(s) could be descendants of anacondas that came to Baltimore in the hulls of fruit ships during the nineteenth century. Is such a thing even possible? John Marriner, head of the Virginia Institute of Marine Science ichthyology department, answered the question in a 1980 *Spartanburg Herald* article. Said Marriner, "I would have to say that's a valid possibility." Obviously, it would be tough for anacondas to survive the winter months in the Mid-Atlantic region. But what if some did and reproduced? Could this explain Chessie sightings?

Many who believe in the existence of sea serpents and lake monsters think they could be something prehistoric that has managed to survive into the present day. With their long necks, plesiosaurs often come to mind. Plesiosaurs were large marine reptiles that thrived during the Jurassic period (about 200 million to 145 million years ago), so obviously, skeptics see this explanation as farfetched. My favorite, albeit improbable, Chessie explanation is the basilosaurus, a long, slender whale from the Eocene epoch (approximately 56 to 34 million years ago). In my mind, basilosauruses are a good fit for modern-day reports of sea serpents.

There are mundane explanations for Chessie, too. The *St. Petersburg Times* ran an article in 1978 in which marine life experts gave their take on the

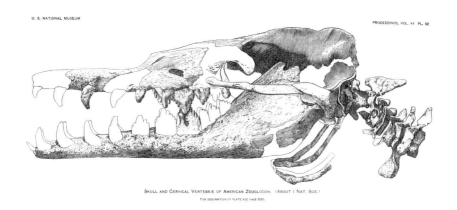

J.W. Gidley's 1913 drawing of the reconstructed skull and neck of a basilosaurus. *Wikimedia Commons.*

Chessie mystery. Dr. Joseph Cooney, then director of the marine biology department at the University of Maryland, said that the existence of an undiscovered animal in the Chesapeake Bay is unlikely. He attributed the bulk of Chessie sightings to porpoises and otters. In the same article, director of the Calvert Marine Museum Dr. Ralph Eshelman said he believed some Chessie sightings might be rays. He said, "I've seen fifty rays with their tails raised stirring up a boil in the water and it looks very strange." Of course, skeptics love to point to logs and floating debris as explanations for Chessie.

MANATEES AND MERMAIDS

Maybe the most popular theory to explain Chessie sightings is wayward manatees passing through the Chesapeake Bay. Though manatees call Florida home, they do make occasional appearances in the Chesapeake during the summer months, drawn there by the bay's abundance of aquatic grass.

A manatee named Chessie visited the Chesapeake Bay several times over a twenty-year period, with the first recorded sighting in 1994. Chessie the manatee was easy to identify. He had a twelve-inch scar running along his left side. (Many manatees are scarred or disfigured, usually from contact with boat propellers.)

Wildlife biologists captured Chessie and placed a radio transmitter on him to track his movements. Chessie gave biologists a scare after his last sighting in Virginia waters in 2001. However, after a lengthy absence, Chessie reappeared in Calvert County, Maryland, in 2011. As of this writing, Chessie is alive and well in Florida and thought to be at least thirty-five years old.

Manatees are large mammals that reach ten feet in length and weigh close to a ton. And sure, not being among the typical wildlife of the Chesapeake Bay, a manatee could be mistaken for something strange. But obviously, manatees do not fit the serpentine characteristics ascribed to Chessie.

Manatees pop up again and again in unexplained phenomena and take the blame for more than Chessie sightings. Tarpie, a water monster in Florida, is a manatee according to some. Many believe a manatee can explain Georgia's water monster, the Altamaha-ha. Kipsy, a river monster in New York, might have been a wayward manatee. These are only a few examples. But in my mind, where manatees shine the brightest in the world of the weird is in tales of mermaids.

Mermaid sightings have long been a staple of maritime lore. In fact, Christopher Columbus had a mermaid sighting on January 9, 1493, off the coast of Hispaniola. Columbus watched three mermaids surface, and he later wrote that they did not possess the beauty that so many attribute to them. Most think it was manatees rather than mermaids that Columbus saw, which would explain his disappointment with their looks.

Colonists and plantation owners in the former Dutch colony of Berbice had tales of mermaids in the rivers. Colin Chisholm recorded an interesting passage in his book *An Essay on the Malignant Pestilential Fever*, published in 1801:

> *The upper portion resembles the human figure, the head smaller in proportion, sometimes bare, but oftener covered with a copious quantity of long black hair. The shoulders are broad, and the breasts large and well formed. The lower portion resembles the tail-portion of a fish, is of immense dimension, the tail forked, and not unlike that of the dolphin, as it is usually represented. The colour of the skin is either black or tawny. The animal is held in veneration and dread by the Indians, who imagine that the killing it would be attended with the most calamitous consequences. It is from this circumstance that none of these animals have been shot, and, consequently, not examined but at a distance. They have been generally observed in a sitting posture in the water, none of the lower extremity being discovered until they are disturbed; when, by plunging, the tail appears, and agitates the water to a considerable distance round. They have been always seen employed in smoothing their hair, or stroking their faces and breasts with their hands, or something resembling hands. In this posture, and thus employed, they have been frequently taken for Indian women bathing.*

Much like the Columbus mermaid sighting, most attribute the old mermaid legends from Berbice to manatees. This makes sense, as many who lived in the Dutch settlements claimed to have eaten the flesh of the river "mermaids."

The legendary John Smith, a leading figure in the establishment of Jamestown in 1607, had a mermaid sighting in the West Indies in 1614. Smith spotted a graceful woman swimming near the shore and wrote:

> *The upper part of her body resembled that of a woman....She had large eyes, rather too round, a finely-shaped nose (a little too short), well-formed ears, rather too long...and her green hair imparted to her an original character by no means unattractive...*[but] *from below the waist the woman gave way to the fish.*

An illustration of John Smith from his work *The Generall Historie of Virginia, New England, and the Summer Isles. Wikimedia Commons.*

Did Smith mistake a manatee for a mermaid? Maybe. But confusing mermaids and manatees has always puzzled me. Equally puzzling to me is the effort skeptics will go through to explain away Chessie sightings. They point to manatees, fish, logs, debris, otters, hoaxers, attention seekers and more. But why? With its vast area and all its water, is it so hard to believe that something undiscovered could be lurking in the Chesapeake Bay?

Chapter 6

OTHER WEIRDOS

Virginia is a land of traditions, and the list of alleged beasts said to be lurking in the state varies widely, from such winged denizens as Snallygasters and Thunderbirds to "Chessie," a thirty-five-foot-long sea monster that is said to patrol the Chesapeake Bay.
—*L.B. Taylor Jr.,*
Monsters of Virginia: Mysterious Creatures in the Old Dominion

I f you have spent much time reading books on cryptozoology and paranormal activity or engaged in social media groups and pages that cover such topics, you might get the idea that Virginia is a weird place. There are thunderbirds in Louisa County; seven-foot-tall, winged humanoids flying over Fredericksburg; bipedal "upright" canines stalking the entire state; a gargoyle in Bluefield; a "deer man" in Tappahannock; Sheepsquatch hiding in southwestern Virginia; and gray aliens that break into bedrooms all over the commonwealth. These are but a few examples of the strange creatures lurking in the shadows. Maybe the weirdest thing I have heard of in Virginia is a creepy, crawling kind of creature that scared the hell out of a Cumberland County bowhunter.

A Crawler in Cumberland County

There is a strange phenomenon taking place within the world of cryptozoology—or if you prefer, this phenomenon is metaphysical in nature. Whether flesh-and-blood, paraphysical or extraterrestrial, sightings of so-called crawlers are just plain weird. Crawlers are humanoid creatures that are tall and lanky with "sunken eyes" and sharp teeth and claws. Crawlers are hairless, and their skin is gray. But here is where they really get weird: witnesses claim that crawlers seem "out of focus" even when close by, and they crawl fast on all fours. Some call crawlers "the world's strangest cryptid." With reports such as this sent through my website, it is easy to see why:

Hey Denver—

I thought you might want to hear about this crazy thing I saw. I used to bowhunt on a few hundred acres in northern Cumberland County. A couple years ago I had hunted all day in early October on a Saturday. I saw a few does and a small six point, but they were all on the far end of comfortable shooting range so I let them go. I left a little earlier than I usually do that evening. I usually sit in my stand until dark, but this time I left while there was a little light left. Anyway, I was heading out on a four-wheeler road. It's about a fifteen-minute walk to my truck, parked at a gate at the edge of a field. About halfway there, I saw something weird moving in the shadows in the woods. At this spot, the woods are fairly open and you can see through the trees pretty good. Not too much underbrush. I stopped and looked for a few seconds to see what it was, and it looked like some naked, tall, skinny guy was crawling. It freaked me out, but I was sort of frozen in place. I kept staring trying to figure out what it was. Plus it was almost dark. I know it don't make sense but it was kind of like looking at a fuzzy picture. But anyway I could tell this thing was grayish and had a bald head. I couldn't really see its eyes, just deep eye sockets. It had fangs. It almost looked like that old black and white Nosferatu movie vampire was crawling around in the woods. Except it didn't have those big ears or funky eyebrows.

I was scared to death. I started running down the road and this weird thing came sort of toward me and then parallel to me keeping pace with me while it was crawling! As I ran I slid an arrow out of my quiver in case this thing jumped on me I figured maybe I could stab it. But the way it was crawling so fast, I didn't think there was any way I could hit it if I stopped and took a shot. I don't know how or when, but I finally got away from it. A little before I got to my truck I didn't see it anymore when I turned and looked for it. I literally threw my bow and the arrow I was carrying in the truck bed and peeled out of there. I've not been back to that place since. I never even went back to get my tree stand. In fact, I've only hunted one other time since. That was in gun season with some buddies and their dogs in the morning and afternoon hours.

I don't blame you if you don't believe me. This is the first time I said anything. I'm afraid if I tell friends or family, they'll put me in a straitjacket. Maybe they should, maybe I am crazy. But I saw what I saw. Sometimes I still get nightmares about that damn thing.

Take care,
Jeff

Jeff and I exchanged a couple of emails. I told him I believed him and he is not alone. Folks all over the country and up in Canada, too, have spotted these frightening creatures. However, I could not offer an explanation for his encounter. That does not mean, of course, that I think there is some sort of crawling humanoid unknown to science lurking in the woods. But I suppose it is possible, especially if these things live underground, as many

What kind of strange creatures are lurking in the forests of Virginia? *Author's collection.*

believe. Maybe a better explanation is that some sort of otherworldly intelligence is projecting thoughts of these monsters into the minds of unsuspecting "eyewitnesses." How or why, I cannot offer a guess. At the end of the day, these crawling weirdos are unexplained, and they might even be unexplainable. I sure hope I never see one.

A Two-Tailed Weirdo

Here we saw for the first and only time a breed of dog known as the Double-Nosed Andean Tiger Hound. The two noses are as cleanly divided as though cut with a knife. About the size of a pointer, it is highly valued for its acute sense of smell and ingenuity in hunting jaguars. It is found only on these plains.
—*Percy Fawcett,* Journey to the Lost City of Z

Once in a while, the National Cryptid Society (NCS) shares a report with me they received through their website. Over the last few years, with permission from the witnesses, the NCS has filled me in on some incredible cases. A few that come to mind include a lizardman in Texas, a pack of werewolves in West Virginia and a sea serpent in Oregon. Though not as spooky as a sea serpent or lizardman, or as intriguing as a werewolf, in 2017, the NCS told me of a creature with two tails in Virginia.

According to a patrol officer who worked at a Yorktown refinery until his retirement in 2012, he spotted a strange animal with two tails about eight times during his employment. A fellow security officer and six other employees spotted the creature, too. Those who saw the animal claim it was about a foot and a half tall and around three and a half feet long. The creature had thick, matted brown fur. Its fur was so long that it concealed its legs and facial features. It also had two tails covered in fur. The animal was a swift runner "with a quick side-to-side wobble."

The patrol officer said he once saw the animal run across the road and head into the river next to the refinery. He also discovered a series of large holes in the ground near areas where he had spotted the animal. Unfortunately, as is so often the case with anomalous reports, no one was able to photograph or film the two-tailed mystery animal.

So, what was this thing? Are we dealing with a new category of cryptid or something else? Though it might be a boring conclusion, I think the details of the case point to an animal with a birth defect. While uncommon, animals such as cats, dogs and other animals with tails have been known to be born with an extra tail—sometimes several tails. The question, then, is what animal, sporting an extra tail, fits the profile? In my opinion, the nutria is the best match.

The patrol officer claimed the two-tailed creature was "about the size of a large beaver." In this regard, a nutria fits. Also, nutrias have long, matted hair. The animal's legs were not visible, and nutrias have short legs. The two-tailed animal left a series of deep holes in the vicinity, and nutrias are semi-aquatic animals that live in burrows along water sources.

Nutrias are invasive species that have taken up residence and established a thriving population in Virginia's Tidewater region. The Virginia Department of Wildlife Resources classifies nutrias as a nuisance species. As such, they do not enjoy the same protections as game animals, and there are no regulations in place regarding killing and trapping them.

Though I lean toward a nutria with a birth defect being the culprit in this case, I can't help but think of Colonel Percy Fawcett's "double-nosed dog." During the early 1900s, Percy Fawcett, a renowned British explorer and adventurer, surveyed remote areas in Bolivia, Peru and Brazil on behalf of the Royal Geographic Society. He claimed to have encountered many unusual creatures during his expeditions, such as giant anacondas, and he knew of folks who had experiences with something fitting descriptions of a long-necked dinosaur. In 1913, Fawcett claimed to have seen unusual dogs in Bolivia with two noses. Of course, no one believed Fawcett at the time, but we now know there is a rare dog breed in Bolivia called the double-nosed Andean tiger hound.

So, is there an uncategorized double-tailed aquatic mammal waiting to be discovered in southeastern Virginia? I doubt it. But I cannot rule it out, either.

DOGMEN

In her book *Hunting the American Werewolf*, Linda Godfrey included a report from Fredericksburg of a "bipedal wolf with gray/red hair." Wrote Godfrey, "The creature was 'sprinting' across the road at the time of the sighting, but switched to all fours when it hit the brush on the other side of the road."

The website Cloaked Hedgehog maintains a map of dogman/werewolf reports. In one of the reports, a person in Middlesex County "sat up in bed and pulled back the curtain" and came face to face with a werewolf. The creature "was covered with dark hair with a very long wolf-like muzzle." It had long teeth, and "its breath was hot and smelled like rotten meat." In another report, a witness in Williamsburg saw something weird while driving: "[It] looked like a huge black dog standing on its back legs off the shoulder at the edge of the woods. It looked to be at least seven feet tall with a huge head, like that of a German Shepard. All the hair was black. The body was tapered at the torso, like what you see in the werewolf movies."

Cloaked Hedgehog also told of a fellow who lived on the "edge of the Great Dismal Swamp" and saw a "beast looking right into his window at him." It had "spittle running down its face" and stood on two legs. The creature had "matted fur and a face almost like a wolf, but other than the snout, very human."

The North American Dogman Project investigated a strange sighting in Gloucester County. A woman woke up in the middle of the night "to the sound of scratching at her rear bedroom window." Whatever made the scratching sound also belted out a "penetrating" howl or screech. The horrible sound seemed to "penetrate her body," and her dogs were "cowering, shaking, and the hair on their backs stood up." The witness left her bedroom and sneaked around the house. Once she reached the back of the house, she peeked around the corner and spotted a wolf-like creature standing on two legs. It was between six and eight feet tall. The hairy peeping Tom had orange eyes; they were either luminescent or perhaps the light from the full moon caused them to shine. The monster saw her and turned around, took a step and stopped. Then it hopped three times, faced her and howled. At that point, the beast "ran/hopped towards a creek" behind her home. She heard a splash as if the creature had dived into the water.

So, what is going on? What are these dog-like creatures that peer into windows? That is the $64,000 question. So far, there are plenty of guesses, but no one knows. With the growing popularity of dogmen on the internet and social media—popularity that is beginning to rival that of Bigfoot—I sometimes wonder if dogmen can be explained by the Recency Effect. The Recency Effect is the principle in which the most recently presented items or experiences will most likely be remembered best. In other words, dogman reports spawn more dogman reports because the descriptions are fresh in the minds of those who have strange encounters.

Many people think these mysterious upright canines are a case of mistaken identity. The most popular answer is that they are variations of Bigfoot creatures. In fact, according to Matt Moneymaker, star of Animal Planet's hit show *Finding Bigfoot*, nearly every unexplained bipedal creature is a misidentified Bigfoot. In August 2017, Moneymaker said this on Twitter after a follower asked for his take on dogman sightings: "Nonsense….Authors twisting bigfoot sightings, at best, to create a new cryptid category. Same for Mothman and Lizardman….All are bigfoots."

Let's face it, seven-foot-tall upright canines cannot exist in nature, so they have to be something else. I have proposed the idea that many dogman sightings could be attributed to kangaroos. You would be shocked at the number of runaway kangaroo sightings in the United States and Europe. Given their size, claws, big ears and long muzzle, I think this makes as much sense as a misidentified Bigfoot. After all, we know kangaroos exist—no one has yet proven that Bigfoot does. All that said, I think many werewolf/ dogman sightings point to something supernatural in nature. For example, the *Daily Mirror* printed this strange account:

> *The family of a fighter pilot who witnessed a UFO say that have seen a "wolf-like" creature that walks on its hind legs stalking their home. The unnamed pilot was onboard the USS* Nimitz *when they sighted the infamous "Tic Tac" encounter, named after the shape of the unidentified aerial phenomena (UAP)….The wife and two teen children of the sailor who investigated the* Nimitz *incident claimed to have seen a wolf-like creature that walked on two hind legs staring into their Virginia home on two occasions.*

In my mind, bizarre encounters such as this, following the sighting of a strange aerial object, point to these creatures being some sort of paranormal entity. And if this is the case, then conventional explanations such as the Recency Effect and runaway kangaroos fall short for the bulk of werewolf and dogman reports.

Chapter 7

URBAN LEGENDS? LET'S HOPE SO!

This was an urban legend that didn't make it on to snopes.com.
—*Jackie Sonnenberg,* All That Glitters

We have all heard various urban legends. And as teenagers, many of our friends dared us to test them. I remember my buddies challenging me to go into the bathroom, turn off the lights and say "Bloody Mary" several times. I was uneasy about it, but peer pressure is a powerful motivator. So I went inside, shut the door, took a deep breath and turned off the lights. I summoned the courage to say "Bloody Mary" three times. I made sure to speak loud enough that my friends could hear me. Of course, nothing happened. Feeling brave, I said it a couple more times, even louder, to let my buddies know Bloody Mary was no match for me. Proud of myself, I flipped the lights back on and turned toward the door. About that time, one of the guys pulled the switch in the breaker box, and the lights went out. The rest of my friends held the bathroom door shut so I couldn't get out, and they started teasing me. They nearly wet their pants from laughing so hard, while I almost wet mine out of fear. The thirty seconds I spent trapped in the dark bathroom felt like an eternity. For a brief moment, I was a Bloody Mary believer.

As a young man, I tested more than a few urban legends, but my friends locking me in the bathroom during a Bloody Mary dare stands out the most. The "fact-checking" website snopes.com says this about urban legends:

Urban legends are, in a basic sense, anecdotes that people share with one another, akin to jokes or tall tales. But although many urban legends are humorous in nature, they typically serve a purpose other than mere entertainment—urban legends offer a framework for imparting warnings, reinforcing moral standards, expressing prejudices, and sharing social anxieties.

Personally, I do not put much stock in snopes.com or so-called fact checkers, for that matter. Nothing kills the social media experience faster than seeing a Facebook post and then reading the smug "this post may be missing context" message. Go away. Who asked you? Besides, is anyone fact-checking the fact checkers? How can we be sure they are correct? What about the biases the fact checkers and their Silicon Valley employers hold? As much as I dislike fact checkers, there are a few stories from Virginia in which I hope they are right. They have to be. Because if they are wrong, there is a werewolf, a vampire and a serial killer in a rabbit costume lurking in the commonwealth.

THE BUNNY MAN

You have probably come across several websites that tell you where to find the most haunted places in Virginia. If so, you have heard of Colchester Overpass in Clifton, better known as Bunny Man Bridge. According to the internet at least, Bunny Man Bridge is a terrifying place. The villainous Bunny Man goes on the prowl at night and has a history of leaving skinned, partially eaten rabbits hanging from trees, killing pets and murdering small children and teenagers.

Countless websites trace the Bunny Man to Douglas J. Grifon, a criminally insane inmate institutionalized for murdering his family on Easter Sunday. Grifon escaped police custody in 1904, setting the stage for the Bunny Man legend. As the story goes, Fairfax County residents petitioned their elected officials to shut down an insane asylum in Clifton. They succeeded in their request, and the criminally insane were transferred to Lorton Prison. During the transfer process, one of the vehicles crashed, killing the driver and most of the inmates. Ten prisoners escaped; police apprehended all but two of them—Marcus A. Wallster and Douglas J. Grifon.

This would be a good place to mention some important facts. First, there was never an insane asylum in Clifton, or in Fairfax County, for that matter.

Second, Lorton Prison was not established until 1910. And third, though Lorton is in Virginia, while the prison was in operation, it only housed inmates from Washington, D.C. In yet another strike against the accuracy of the story, neither Grifon nor Wallster appears in the court records of Fairfax County.

Continuing with the internet version of events, authorities searched for Grifon and Wallster for months. During the search, police and locals found mutilated rabbits hanging from trees and rabbit body parts scattered throughout the woods. Eventually, police found Wallster; his lifeless, mutilated corpse was hanging from Colchester Overpass. Police recovered a note pinned on Wallster's foot that read, "You'll never find me no matter how hard you try! Signed, The Bunny Man."

The authorities finally caught up with Grifon and located him at the Colchester Overpass. Before they could take him into custody, an oncoming train ran over Grifon, killing him. Moments after his demise, police heard Grifon laughing.

Naturally, there are variations of the story on the internet. In some accounts, police did not apprehend Grifon, nor was he killed by a passing train. Instead, Grifon remained on the loose and preyed on unsuspecting teenagers at the Colchester Overpass.

Probably the most widely circulated version of the Bunny Man tale, titled "The Clifton Bunny Man" by Timothy C. Forbes, appeared on the website Castle of Spirits in 1999. According to Forbes, on Halloween 1905, some kids were partying at the Colchester Overpass. A bright light shined, and an instant later, they were dead. Forbes wrote:

> *Not only were their throats slashed, but all up and down their chests were long slashes gutting them. To top it off the Bunny Man hung both of the guys from one end of a bridge with a rope around their neck, hanging from the overpass with their legs dangling in front of the pass of cars. The women were hung the same way on the other side of the bridge.*

The next year on Halloween, Bunny Man struck again. According to Forbes:

> *That night seven teens were left remaining right before midnight at the bridge. Thinking little of it, six remained inside the bridge while Adrian Hatala had remained a good distance from the bridge hoping to have enough time to escape if the same thing happened again. At midnight she witnessed*

only this, a dim light walking the railroad track right before midnight, stopping right above the bridge at midnight, then disappearing at the same time as a bright flash was inside the bridge. She heard the deafening sounds of horrific screams coming from inside the bridge that lasted only seconds. Five seconds later, they were all hung from the edge of the bridge, same style as the corpses a year earlier.

According to the Forbes story, police arrested Hatala for the murders and sent her to Lorton. However, authorities later cleared her of wrongdoing after someone murdered nine teenagers at Bunnyman Bridge in 1913.

Supposedly, there were others who met their end at Colchester Overpass. In 1949 and again in 1976, police discovered mutilated bodies of teenagers hanging beneath the bridge.

Needless to say, there is no record of the bloodshed at Colchester Overpass either in local newspapers or in official police records. So if the murders cannot be verified and if key elements of the Bunny Man's backstory are demonstrably false, why is Bunny Man Bridge so renowned for its "hauntings"? Why is Bunny Man so popular on the internet? Is there a real story behind the legend?

As it turns out, there was a deranged rabbit man prowling Fairfax County in 1970. On October 22, 1970, the *Washington Post* ran an article titled "Man in Bunny Suit Sought in Fairfax." The article reads:

Fairfax County police said yesterday they are looking for a man who likes to wear "white bunny rabbit costume" and throw hatchets through car windows. Honest.

Air Force Academy Cadet Robert Bennett told police that shortly after midnight last Sunday he and his fiancée were sitting in a car in the 5400 block of Guinea Road when a man "dressed in a white suit with long bunny ears" ran from the nearby bushes and shouted: "You're on private property and I have your tag number."

The "rabbit" threw a wooden-handled hatchet through the right front car window, the first-year cadet told police. As soon as he threw the hatchet, the "rabbit" skipped off into the night, police said. Bennett and his fiancée were not injured.

Police say they have the hatchet, but no other clues in the case. They say Bennett was visiting an uncle, who lives across the street from the spot where the car was parked. The cadet was in the area to attend last weekend's Air Force–Navy football game.

The rabbit man made a reappearance a week and a half later. On October 31, 1970, the *Washington Post* reported:

> *A man wearing a furry rabbit suit with two long ears appeared—again— on Guinea Road in Fairfax County Thursday night, police reported, this time wielding an ax and chopping away at a roof support on a new house.*
>
> *Less than two weeks ago a man wearing what was described as a rabbit suit accused two persons in a parked car of trespassing and heaved a hatchet through a closed window of the car at 5400 Guinea Rd. They were not hurt.*
>
> *Thursday night's rabbit, wearing a suit described as gray, black and white, was spotted a block away at 5307 Guinea Rd.*
>
> *Paul Phillips, a private security guard for a construction company, said he saw the "rabbit" standing on the front porch of a new, but unoccupied house.*
>
> *"I started talking to him," Phillips said, "and that's when he started chopping."*
>
> *"All you people trespass around here," Phillips said the "rabbit" told him as he whacked eight gashes in the pole. "If you don't get out of here, I'm going to bust you on the head."*
>
> *Phillips said he walked back to his car to get his handgun, but the "rabbit," carrying the long-handled ax, ran off into the woods.*
>
> *The security guard said the man was about 5-feet-8, 160 pounds and appeared to be in his early 20s.*

The Fairfax County Police Department responded to the incident. They sent officers to Guinea Road to look for "a subject dressed as a rabbit with an axe." Police found no trace of the bunny, and the department handed the case over to W.L. Johnson of the Criminal Investigation Bureau.

Johnson received a call from a worker at the subdivision where the Bunny Man was last seen. The caller had received a phone call from someone claiming to be the "Axe Man." The Axe Man said, "You have been messing up my property, by dumping tree stumps, limbs and brush, and other things on the property. You can make everything right by meeting me tonight and talking about the situation." Police staked out the location, but the "Axe Man" failed to show up.

Johnson received tips from local residents claiming to know the identity of Bunny Man, but these were dead ends. Most of the leads were rumors from schoolchildren who had been talking back and forth. The case went cold, and Johnson wrote the following on March 14, 1971:

After a very extensive investigation into this and all other cases of this same nature, it is still unsubstantiated as to whether or not there really is a white rabbit.

The only people who have seen this so-called white rabbit have been children of rather young ages, and the complainant in this case.

Upon interviewing everyone in this case that may have had any knowledge of any incidents concerning a white rabbit, that has been no significant information uncovered that would lead to the identity of the person or persons that were posing as a white rabbit.

This case will be marked as inactive.

Police never apprehended the Bunny Man; this undoubtedly helped fuel the legend. Bunny Man sightings spread throughout Fairfax County and made their way into Washington, D.C., the Maryland suburbs and as far away as Culpeper, Virginia, about sixty miles southwest of Clifton. From a strange man dressed in a rabbit costume—probably upset over rapid housing development—the story morphed into a criminally insane serial killer from the early 1900s. Call me crazy, but I have always believed the real

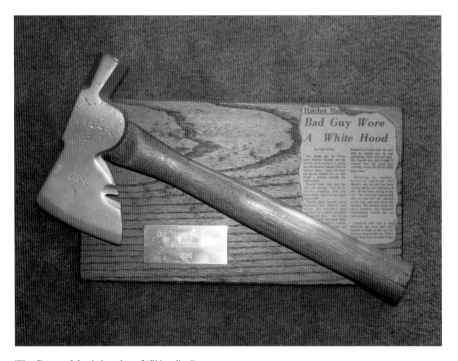

The Bunny Man's hatchet. *Wikimedia Commons.*

story of the Bunny Man is better than the embellished internet tales. Think about it: a grown man in a rabbit costume with an axe running through a construction site threatening people. You don't need the fake backstory—that is scary enough!

Today, the Colchester Overpass, or Bunny Man Bridge, is an attraction for road trippers and paranormal enthusiasts. I've been there myself many years ago, and quite frankly, the tiny bridge was a little disappointing. If you decide to visit, do not go on Halloween night. Not because of the Bunny Man, but I've been told police set up checkpoints during the Halloween season and turn away nonresidents. But who knows? That might be an urban legend, too.

A Vampire and a Werewolf

The Richmond area is home to stories of both a werewolf and a vampire. A werewolf and a vampire—that makes me think of the *Twilight* series of books and movies. For those unfamiliar, "the series explores the unorthodox romance between human Bella and vampire Edward, as well as the love triangle between Bella, Edward, and Jacob, a werewolf," according to Wikipedia. As a fifty-year-old man, it is embarrassing to acknowledge my familiarity with *Twilight*, but during the height of its popularity, my daughters were rabid fans. One was on "Team Edward," and the other was in the "Team Jacob" camp. After listening to my daughters debate which is sexier, a werewolf or a vampire, my mind is forever scarred.

If you type the word *werewolf* into an internet search engine, it will not take long until the search results lead you to the Henrico Werewolf, a six-foot-tall humanoid with a "wolf-like" face. The creature inhabits the Springs Recreation Center, formerly called Confederate Hills Recreation Center, in Henrico County, just east of Richmond. Some say the dog-like creature is covered in gray fur, but according to most accounts, its hair is black and tipped in a silvery color. The werewolf howls at night and, as you might have guessed, is most active during a full moon. Though the monster stands and walks upright, at times it drops down on all fours and runs like a typical canine. This usually occurs when someone notices the creature or gets too close.

In a lot of ways, the Henrico Werewolf seems to fit into the modern dogman phenomenon, with one exception—it does not seem to be malevolent. In fact, some have described the werewolf as "almost playful." It intentionally goes near people but makes sure not to get too close. Stories of the creature have been around long before dogmen became popular; some even say the werewolf can be traced to the Civil War. In this origin story, the Henrico Werewolf is the manifestation of a Civil War soldier who chose the form of a werewolf to keep people away from him. Paranormal investigator Jake Fife, in an interview with VPM News, said that many folks believe "the spirit mimics the form of what Virginians call dogmen." In the interview, Fife said that he believed the Henrico Werewolf is a hoax and pointed to the fact that dogmen were not widely reported prior to the early 2000s.

I am not sure I would go as far as to call the Henrico Werewolf a hoax. I would, however, place it in the urban legend category.

I would also call the Richmond Vampire an urban legend. Also known as the Hollywood Vampire, the creature resides in Richmond's Hollywood Cemetery. Hollywood Cemetery is adjacent to the campus of Virginia Commonwealth University (VCU) and holds a number of notable burials, including two United States presidents, James Monroe and John Tyler. Jefferson Davis, president of the Confederate States of America, is also buried in Hollywood Cemetery.

W.W. Pool is also a significant burial in Hollywood Cemetery—not for anything the bookkeeper did in his life but because decades after his death, he became Richmond's version of Dracula. William Wortham Pool built a tomb for his wife, Alice, who died in 1913 "after an illness of several weeks." Pool passed away in 1922 at the age of eighty and was laid to rest next to Alice. Pool was buried with full Masonic rites, and interestingly, his mausoleum features Masonic and Egyptian motifs. These elements with their inherent mystique, as well as the initials W.W. on the mausoleum, which some people think resemble fangs, have contributed to the vampire lore surrounding W.W. Pool.

Rumors of strange activity in Hollywood Cemetery took hold during the 1950s and 1960s. As time went on, tales spread of mysterious occult rituals taking place at W.W. Pool's tomb. On Halloween night, intruders would break into the cemetery and chant and perform incantations at Pool's mausoleum. But many think these are nothing more than tales started by VCU students.

Where did the idea of a vampire in Hollywood Cemetery come from? This is a tough question to answer, but some trace the vampire to 1925 and the tragic collapse of the Church Hill Tunnel. The Chesapeake and Ohio (C&O) Railway built the Church Hill Tunnel in the early 1870s beneath Richmond's Church Hill district. The tunnel, about three-quarters of a mile in length, collapsed on October 2, 1925, trapping a steam locomotive and ten railcars. Rescue efforts failed and further weakened the tunnel. Four men died in the collapse.

Legend holds that shortly after the Church Hill Tunnel collapsed, rescue workers saw a hideous creature crouched over a victim. It was covered in blood and gore with partially decomposed folds of skin hanging from its emaciated body. Blood was dripping from the monster's mouth and chin, and it had jagged teeth. The creature fled the scene and headed in the direction of Hollywood Cemetery. A group followed the monster and saw it enter the tomb of W.W. Pool.

A couple of things from the story seem unlikely to me, the first being that W.W. Pool was some sort of undead creature awakened by the collapse of the tunnel. It also does not seem plausible that rescue workers would shift their efforts from trying to locate and help the injured to pursuing a vampire-like creature over a distance of a couple of miles. Where does the truth lie?

Researcher Gregory Maitland with the Richmond-based paranormal research group Night Shift offered an explanation for the supposed creature in the tunnel. He said Benjamin F. Mosby was the only worker who made it out of the tunnel. Mosby had been shoveling coal into the firebox of the steam locomotive when the boiler tank ruptured in the collapse. Mosby was severely scalded and had flaps of skin "measuring up to four inches in width" hanging from his body. He also had several broken teeth and cuts all over his body from crawling out of the tunnel. When rescue workers found Mosby, he was in a state of shock. Mosby asked the rescue workers to contact his wife and tell her he was alive. Mosby later died in the hospital from his wounds, and he is buried in Hollywood Cemetery. According to Maitland, it was Mosby and his horrific wounds that inspired the Richmond Vampire legend.

THE VANISHING HITCHHIKER

The "vanishing hitchhiker" is one of our most enduring urban legends. The vanishing hitchhiker—alternately called phantom hitchhiker, disappearing hitchhiker and ghostly hitchhiker, to name a few—typically stands alongside a road at night looking for a ride. An unsuspecting motorist will stop and give the hitchhiker a ride, and often the hitchhiker will simply vanish. Other times, the hitchhiker will have a conversation with the driver and reveal a personal detail from the driver's life and depart the vehicle in the normal manner after reaching his or her destination. Some hitchhikers leave something behind in the vehicle, such as an article of clothing.

Volumes have been written on this phenomenon, and those who think they understand it have put forth countless theories to explain away the ghostly hitchhikers. But to me, mainstream explanations fall short, even more so when I reflect on a strange experience I had in 2002. I was driving north on U.S. 29 between Elkwood, Virginia, and Remington, Virginia, at about 3:45 a.m. At that time of night, I had the road to myself other than the occasional eighteen-wheeler across the median in the southbound lanes. As always when out at that hour, I was listening to a weird talk radio show on a staticky AM station. Out of nowhere, a man materialized in front of my truck. I was barreling down on him at over sixty miles per hour; he was in my lane walking in a diagonal direction with his head down. He never looked up or changed his pace.

I slammed the brakes, held down the horn and let fly an assortment of expletives that would embarrass Samuel L. Jackson. My truck fishtailed as I narrowly missed the late-night jaywalker. For good measure, I screamed several more profanities at him as I began shaking uncontrollably. Right about then, things turned weird.

I barely missed him, yet when I looked through my mirrors, I couldn't see him. He was gone. I rolled my window down and stuck my head out and looked around—he wasn't anywhere to be found. He was not in the median, in the road or anywhere—he had vanished.

I still remember what the man looked like. He wore faded blue jeans and a gray pocket T-shirt. It looked like he had a pack of cigarettes in the shirt pocket. He was over six feet tall with sandy-colored hair. His straight hair hung below his shoulders, and it was short on the top and sides—the infamous mullet hairstyle, "all business in the front and a party in the back." This fellow looked straight out of 1991; he even had the sleeves of his T-shirt rolled up midway to his shoulder.

I pulled over onto the shoulder of the road long enough to collect myself. Who was this guy? My first thought was that he was strung out on some sort of hallucinogenic drug, but that did not make sense. There was not a house anywhere around that he could have been coming from. There were no broken-down cars anywhere either. Even if he were out of his mind from drugs, I could not explain him being where he was—or how he appeared out of nowhere and then vanished. I then started thinking maybe he was trying to kill himself—suicide by car. But then, if he really wanted to kill himself, why not walk north a mile or two and jump off the bridge into the Rappahannock River? And again, how did he do his disappearing act? Nothing added up, and it still doesn't.

The experience troubled me for a while, but I eventually pushed it into the back of my mind. I did not tell anyone; in fact, a 2020 post on my blog was the first time I mentioned it. In 2021, I recounted the story to Jeremy Socha, host of the *Infinite Rabbit Hole* podcast, when I was a guest on the show. He asked if I had ever done any investigating to find out if maybe someone died there in the past. I told him I had not, and I still haven't. Truthfully, I am not sure if I want to know. It was a strange experience; I suppose I was at the right place at the right time, and it just happened. I don't know what to make of it, but I will say that when folks speak of their vanishing hitchhiker tales, I am not quick to try to debunk them or write them off as urban legends. Anything is possible at three o'clock in the morning on Virginia's highways.

PART II
BURIED TREASURE

Chapter 8

COLONIAL GOLD

Buried treasure isn't worth much.
—*S.R. Ford,* Mimgardr

Virginia has a long history. It all began with the Charter of 1606, when King James I assigned land rights in North America to the Virginia Company for colonization. The king's logic was simple—a colony would deter Spanish encroachment and provide economic opportunity for colonists and the Crown. In 1607, English colonists left their homes, crossed the sea and established the settlement of Jamestown. It did not take long for English settlements to spread along the James River and, soon afterward, beyond.

The English had tried colonizing North America before; however, the Virginia Colony was the first to survive. In 1583, Sir Humphrey Gilbert made an ill-fated attempt at setting up a colony in Newfoundland. Shortly thereafter, Humphrey's half brother, Sir Walter Raleigh, tried to establish a colony on Roanoke Island in present-day Dare County, North Carolina. But it was not meant to be. By 1590, all that remained of the colony were the letters "CRO" scratched into a tree and the word "CROATOAN" carved into a post. Now over 430 years later, we still do not know what happened to the Roanoke Colony, earning it the nickname the Lost Colony.

Unlike previous failures, the Virginia Colony made it, and the settlement at Jamestown survived. But it was not easy. Early on, Jamestown was on the brink of collapse until new settlers and precious supplies arrived in 1610.

RUINS OF THE ENGLISH SETTLEMENT
AT ROANOKE.

John White at the ruins of the Roanoke Colony in 1590. This engraving by John Parker Davis is from the 1893 book *Columbus and Columbia: A Pictorial History of the Man and the Nation. Wikimedia Commons.*

From 1610 to 1614, war with the Powhatan Confederacy threatened the young colony. Tensions eased for a time when tobacco cultivation pioneer John Rolfe married Pocahontas, the daughter of Chief Powhatan. By the early 1620s, the uneasy peace had declined, and relations between the Powhatan and colonists reached their boiling point. To try to satisfy an insatiable demand for the Crown's lucrative new cash crop, tobacco, colonists pushed deeper and deeper into Powhatan lands. Sprawling plantations lined both sides of the James River and stretched for miles on end. But it wasn't enough.

When Chief Powhatan died, his younger brother Opechancanough succeeded him. The new chief intended to put an end to the never-ending English expansion. In the spring of 1622, he launched a series of attacks against English settlements and plantations along the James River. Opechancanough and his warriors struck over thirty locations and wiped out several communities. In total, 347 colonists died in the raids—a staggering one-quarter of the colony's population. The attacks came to be known as the Jamestown massacre.

Hostilities between the colonists and Powhatan raged on for more than two decades. In 1644, Opechancanough orchestrated another set of major attacks, this time killing around five hundred colonists. In harsh reprisals, the English killed hundreds of Powhatans. By 1646, decades of war and disease had nearly wiped out the Powhatan tribes, and a treaty dissolved

Above: Matthaeus Merian's 1628 woodcut depicting the Jamestown massacre. *National Park Service.*

Left: An engraving of Captain John Smith taking Opechancanough prisoner in 1608. *Maryland State Archives.*

the Powhatan Confederacy. What was left of the Powhatan tribes either relocated or were confined to land that would go on to become Indian reservations. Two of the Powhatan tribes, the Mattaponi and Pamunkey, still live on reservations in King William County carved out in the seventeenth century.

In his book *10 Treasure Legends!: Virginia*, author and professional treasure hunter J. Hutton Pulitzer hinted that a vast amount of treasure is buried along the James River. He noted the habit of early colonists burying their money on their property. Said Pulitzer, "Families still buried their money below ground on their plantations. While it is expected to be quite large, it is unknown just how great a fortune is buried underground along the banks of the James River." Pulitzer may be on to something. If over a quarter of the population of the Colony of Virginia died in the 1622 Jamestown massacre, what became of their coins and valuables? And what of those who died in the 1644 attacks? Many of those killed were wealthy tobacco planters. Given the gold and silver exchange rates today, the monetary value of these hidden caches could be mind boggling.

Gold in Centreville?

In February 1755, as the French and Indian War raged in North America, British general Edward Braddock landed in Hampton with two regiments and supplies for the war effort. In April, Braddock attended the Congress of Alexandria, where he met with five colonial governors to secure financial backing for actions against the French. During the meeting, it was decided that Braddock would lead an expedition to Fort Duquesne in present-day Pittsburgh. Shortly thereafter, provincial troops joined Braddock's force, and they began their march to the fort through the early American wilderness.

The Braddock expedition encountered trouble right away. Snowmelt and April showers had turned their route into an impassable river of mud and muck. By the time Braddock reached Newgate—renamed Centreville in 1792—he had become desperate. Braddock had brought twelve artillery pieces along, including four howitzers, four twelve-pound cannons and four six-pound cannons. In an effort to lighten his load, he decided to bury a couple of his cannons. He took two of the six-pounders and buried them facing skyward and then filled them with gold coins. The coins were part of the expedition payroll and valued at $30,000. Braddock sealed the cannon bores with wooden plugs and planned to retrieve them when he returned.

In this drawing, General Edward Braddock, wounded at the Battle of Monongahela, is transported to safety. He later died of his wounds. *Project Gutenberg*

Braddock carefully recorded the location of the stash in his notes: "Fifty paces east of a spring where the road runs north and south."

Braddock did not make it back. After a taxing march, he suffered a crushing defeat at the Battle of Monongahela, about ten miles from Fort Duquesne. Braddock's devastating loss takes the dubious distinction of being one of the worst defeats the British suffered in the eighteenth century. Braddock was mortally wounded in the battle, and his force suffered a tremendous number of casualties. Braddock's last words were, "Who would have thought?"

None of the survivors of the disastrous campaign had knowledge of the buried gold back in Newgate, giving birth to a treasure legend. According to Chas J. Gilliss, who wrote an article for the *Historical Society of Fairfax County, Virginia, Inc. Yearbook* in 1954, after Braddock died, military personnel sent his notes and papers to England. Wrote Gilliss:

> *And so it was, that not until many years after, when interest began to revive in this ill-fated expeditions, led by Braddock…that an archivist, in going over the papers, discovered by accident the secret of this buried treasure. A committee was sent from England to Centreville to search for the spring, which was to give the clue, but though they spent some time in the locality, no spring could be found which gave promise of the exact spot.*

Gilliss believed urban development in Centreville caused the spring to dry up. He is probably right. Even if there is gold buried in Centreville, how would one go about finding "a spring where the road runs north and south"? According to Gilliss, the British government, which claimed ownership of the loot, offered "one half of the gold to anyone who finds it."

This is quite a story, and it is fascinating to think British gold is buried—stored in cannons, no less—somewhere under the traffic, houses and strip malls in Centreville. According to the CPI Inflation Calculator, the $30,000 cache would be worth about $1,480,855 today. However, that figure is conservative, as gold values have far outpaced the rate of inflation. According to the website Only Gold, in 1792, the price of gold stood at $19.39 an ounce. Using that figure, the gold coins in question would make up around 1,547 ounces. As I write the words, an ounce of gold is worth $1,816, putting the value of the treasure at $2,809,352. Of course, there may have been silver coins mixed in, too, but silver has also outperformed the rate of inflation.

Not everyone agrees that Braddock buried treasure in Centreville. In fact, in an essay disputing the legend, Douglas Philips and Barnaby Nygren asserted that Braddock did not pass through Centreville at all but rather used a more northerly route on his march to Fort Duquesne. The pair claimed the legend began with the 1954 Gilliss article, and they made a compelling case that Braddock did not leave cannons full of coins under the pavement in Centreville. They conceded, however, that Braddock may have left treasure elsewhere. They wrote, "Local legends, handed down from generation to generation, tell of gold being buried by Braddock somewhere in the hills west of Winchester." They could be right, but for what it's worth, I lived in the Winchester area for fifteen years and never heard anyone mention Braddock's gold lying in the hills west of town.

Philips and Nygren pointed to Wills Creek in western Maryland as another possible location of Braddock's gold. They claimed Braddock ran

Did General Edward Braddock hide gold at Fort Cumberland, Maryland, rather than Centreville, Virginia? *Wikimedia Commons.*

into trouble a day after leaving Fort Cumberland due to "bad roads and weak horses." The expedition had so much difficulty that Braddock called a meeting with his officers. On Braddock's orders, "two six-pounders, four coehorns, and some powder stores were sent back to Fort Cumberland."

In the final analysis, Philips and Nygren did not believe there was any buried treasure tied to Braddock in Centreville, Winchester, western Maryland or anywhere else. They said that the French captured $25,000 in coins after defeating the British and thwarting their plans to capture Fort Duquesne.

What is the truth? I am not sure the truth matters in this case. I like to think that Gilliss was right, rather than Philips and Nygren, and two cannons full of gold are buried in Centreville. But does it matter? Even if you thought you knew where to find them, how could you recover the loot in the midst of all the development in Centreville?

The Bruton Vault

And when he had opened the seventh seal, there was silence in heaven about the space of half an hour.
—Revelation 8:1 (King James Version)

According to legend, a vault containing the lost works of Sir Francis Bacon is buried beneath the Bruton Parish church in Colonial Williamsburg. Sir Francis Bacon (1561–1626) is an interesting character. Bacon was a statesman, philosopher and father of the scientific method. He has also been called "the true founder of America and guardian of her history," "founder of Freemasonry" and "guiding light of the Rosicrucian Order." Additionally, many believe that it was Bacon who wrote the plays attributed to William Shakespeare. Another theory suggests Bacon was the mastermind behind a group of intellectuals that authored the Shakespearean plays. In her book *Foundations Unearthed*, Marie Bauer Hall wrote:

> It is revealed that in the authorship of the Shakespeare plays were concerned not one, or two or three persons, but a group of the greatest intellects of the times. The guiding genius of this group was Sir Francis Bacon; among his associates were such men as Lancelot Andrews, the great Anglican Archbishop; Toby Mathews; John Donne; Ben Jonson; Edmund Spencer; Sir Walter Raleigh; Francis Drake; George Withers, and many others.

Knowing that Bacon may have been the genius behind the works of Shakespeare, it stands to reason that lost Shakespearean works compose part of the loot in the Bruton vault. But that is not all. There are lost books of the Bible, maps to secret vaults in Europe, crown jewels, gold coins and Bacon's blueprint for a utopian society, or a "New Atlantis." Some have deemed Bacon's works to be of such importance to humankind they have compared them to the opening of the seventh seal in the Book of Revelation.

Marie Bauer Hall, wife of influential freemason Manly P. Hall, learned of the Bruton vault and its location through cryptic messages Bacon allegedly placed in Shakespearean and other writings. In 1940, she published a book titled *Foundations Unearthed* in which she detailed her search for the vault. That search led her to Williamsburg, where a ten-foot cubical vault lay sixteen feet below the Bruton Parish Episcopal Church. In 1938, church authorities granted her permission to dig for the vault. Her background work in interpreting Bacon's clues—coded in the writings of William Shakespeare and George Wither—told her the vault was ninety feet northwest of the church door. The location was also near the grave of Ann Graham—another clue given its similarity to the word *anagram*.

Long story short, the church stopped Hall's dig at around a depth of nine feet out of fear of disturbing graves in the churchyard. Local authorities conspired to keep Hall from conducting further excavations. But that was not the end of the digging. In 1991, authorities caught "New Age mystic" Marsha Middleton and two accomplices digging on church property. A local judge ordered the trio not to set foot in Virginia again. The illegal dig prompted church authorities to allow archaeologists to conduct an excavation in 1992, retracing Hall's steps. Sadly, the effort failed to yield results that would prove the existence of the vault. But maybe it was not meant to; many think the excavation was nothing but a sham. To this day, the vault and the lost works of Sir Francis Bacon remain hidden.

Sadly, I think the bulk of buried colonial-era treasure is not recoverable. As mentioned earlier, even if you thought you had a shot at locating Braddock's gold in Centreville, you would have to tear up a parking lot, road, apartment complex or restaurant to get to it. Obviously, that is not happening. The aforementioned small caches along the James River are the proverbial needle in the haystack. It would take a miraculous stroke of dumb luck to even find a place worth digging. In the case of the Bruton vault, I do not believe the powers that be will ever allow its recovery. Think about it this way—why would the global elites want a utopian society or New Atlantis? Things are working out well for them already. The late great comedian and social critic George Carlin said it best in a classic stand-up routine:

> *They spend billions of dollars every year lobbying, lobbying, to get what they want. Well, we know what they want. They want more for themselves and less for everybody else....It's a big club, and you ain't in it. You and I are not in the big club. And by the way, it's the same big club they use to beat you over the head with all day long when they tell you what to believe. All day long beating you over the head with their media telling you what to believe, what to think and what to buy. The table is tilted, folks.*

Chapter 9

PIRATE'S BOOTY

Gold is most excellent, gold is treasure, and he who possesses it does all he wishes to in this world, and succeeds in helping souls into Paradise.
—Christopher Columbus

A ccording to legend, a sailor turned pirate from South Carolina named Charles Wilson buried treasure worth more than $11,500,000 in Chincoteague, Virginia. The tale goes back to 1750, when authorities arrested Wilson for piracy and hanged him for his crimes. While Wilson was in jail, he wrote the following letter to his brother:

> *To My Brother, George Wilson,*
> *There are three creeks lying 100 paces or more north of the second inlet above Chincoteague Island, Virginia, which is at the southward end of the peninsula. At the head of the third creek to the northward is a bluff facing the Atlantic Ocean with three cedar trees growing on it, each about 1.5 yards apart. Between the trees I buried ten iron bound chests, bars of silver, gold, diamonds and jewels to the sum of 200,000 pounds sterling. Go to the woody knoll secretly and remove the treasure.*

The letter was seized before it reached George Wilson, and to this day, the loot remains unclaimed.

Many think the Wilson story is a hoax, while others are firm believers. Most who believe Wilson left a cache behind think it is buried near the

While there might be treasure buried on Assateague Island, it is best known for its wild ponies. *Author's collection.*

A wild pony on Assateague Island. *Author's collection.*

The view from atop the Assateague Lighthouse in Chincoteague, Virginia. *Author's collection.*

The author on the Piankatank River in Gloucester County. Tidal rivers such as this made perfect getaways for pirates. *Author's collection.*

Maryland line on Assateague Island. If true, the story might as well be a hoax. Assateague Island is federally owned except for the 855 acres that make up Maryland's Assateague State Park. The U.S. Fish and Wildlife Service and National Park Service manage the rest of the island. Treasure hunting on federal land is a big no-no. Digging is a felony. You would probably be better off getting caught engaging in piracy than metal detecting on Assateague Island.

Charles Wilson's story is just one of Virginia's many pirate treasure tales. From roughly 1680 to 1730, pirates plagued the Virginia coast. They lurked in Virginia waters and robbed ships transporting tobacco and other cargo. They even attacked ports and harbors. Virginia's waterways with their many inlets, bays and rivers were perfect for small, agile pirate ships. The sea bandits hit their targets and made quick getaways using the maze of inlets. Many notable pirates sailed through Virginia's waters, and some left gold buried on the shore. Perhaps the most famous to do so was Blackbeard.

BLACKBEARD'S TREASURE

Come all you jolly sailors
You all so stout and brave;
Come hearken and I'll tell you
What happen'd on the wave.
Oh! 'tis of that bloody Blackbeard
I'm going now for to tell;
And as how by gallant Maynard
He soon was sent to hell.
—*Benjamin Franklin (attributed)*

Blackbeard was a devilish man and might have been the most ruthless pirate to sail the seas. Born Edward Teach in England, he earned the nickname Blackbeard from his distinctive facial hair that covered his entire face. His unruly beard ran from his eyes all the way down to his stomach. He tied strands of his beard into tails held in place by ribbons and tucked them behind his ears. In battle, Blackbeard lit matches and stuck them under his hat for theatrical effect. According to accounts from the day, "His eyes, naturally looking fierce and wild, made him altogether such a figure that imagination cannot form an idea of a fury from hell to look more frightful."

Blackbeard sailed into the Chesapeake Bay from the Bahamas and used its many inlets to evade detection. He used the bays and creeks near Cape Charles to lie in wait for unsuspecting cargo ships. He was a true menace to commerce and trade.

In June 1718, Blackbeard set up operations in the Outer Banks of North Carolina. This was a little too close to Virginia waters for Governor Alexander Spotswood; he did not want Blackbeard anywhere near Virginia. When Spotswood learned Blackbeard was staying on Ocracoke Island, he decided it was time to end the pirate's reign of terror. Despite Ocracoke being outside his jurisdiction, Spotswood sent Lieutenant Robert Maynard of the HMS *Pearl* after Blackbeard.

Maynard and his crew found the fabled pirate at Ocracoke Island. As Maynard drew closer to Blackbeard's vessel, the pirate asked, "Damn you for villains, who are you? And, from whence came you?"

Maynard replied, "You may see by our colors we are no pirates."

Blackbeard then yelled, "Send your boat on board, that I might see who you are!"

A drawing of the fierce pirate Edward Teach, better known as Blackbeard. *Library of Congress.*

Maynard said that he could not spare his boat but that he intended to board Blackbeard's ship as soon as he could with his sloop. Hearing that, Blackbeard vowed, "Damnation seize my soul if I give you quarters, or take any from you."

Maynard had the same thought and replied, "I expect no quarter, nor shall I give any."

The stage was set for a historic showdown. As Maynard approached Blackbeard's ship, the pirate unleashed a volley of cannon and small arms fire on the sloop. This killed six of Maynard's crew and wounded ten others. Maynard ordered all but a few of his men to go below the ship's deck to protect themselves against another round of fire as they approached the pirates. When Maynard's ship was within reach, Blackbeard, thinking he had killed most of Maynard's men, boarded the enemy vessel with his crew. At that point, Maynard signaled his men to come to the deck, and vicious hand-to-hand combat ensued. The *Boston News-Letter* gave this summary of the battle:

Maynard and Teach themselves begun the fight with their swords, Maynard making a thrust, the point of his sword against Teach's cartridge box, and bent it to the hilt. Teach broke the guard of it, and wounded Maynard's fingers but did not disable him, whereupon he jumped back and threw away his sword and fired his pistol which wounded Teach. Demelt struck in between them with his sword and cut Teach's face pretty much; in the interim both companies engaged in Maynard's sloop. Later during the battle, while Teach was loading his pistol he finally died from blood loss. Maynard then cut off his head and hung it from his bow.

Maynard sailed back to Virginia with the head of Blackbeard swinging from his ship's bowsprit. When he reached Virginia, Blackbeard's head was hung from a pole along the Hampton River as a warning to pirates. The location is known today as Blackbeard's Point.

Maynard brought fifteen of Blackbeard's crew back to Virginia as prisoners, and a court of admiralty tried them in Williamsburg. The court convicted and hanged thirteen of the pirates.

If the legends are true, Blackbeard left treasure behind on Mulberry Island in Newport News. A Portuguese pirate who sailed with Blackbeard named Antonio Silvestro told fellow crew member John Plantain of treasure Blackbeard buried in Virginia. When the two were together in Madagascar, Silvestro gave Plantain the details. Wrote Plantain, "He informed me that if it should be my lot ever to go to an island called Mulberry Island that there the pirates had buried considerable sums of money in great chests, well clamped with iron plates." The location of the loot was at "the upper end of a small sandy covet, where it is convenient to land....Fronting the landing place are five trees among which he said, the money was hid."

So far, no one has found the legendary pirate's loot. According to Blackbeard, it belongs to the devil. He said, "The Devil knows where I've hid it; and the longest liver of the twain will get it all."

Hog Island

Hog Island is one of Virginia's barrier islands, a seventy-mile chain of twenty-three islands along the Eastern Shore. These islands, most of which are uninhabited, help protect the coast from storms. Hog Island is uninhabited today and owned by the Nature Conservancy, but this has not always been the case. English settlers began colonizing Hog Island in the seventeenth century, and the island remained populated until the 1930s, when shoreline erosion forced the last residents to pack up for the mainland.

A small island off the Virginia coast settled in the 1600s is a perfect setting for tales of lost treasure. And it is only fitting that the legendary pirate Captain William Kidd might have buried his loot on Hog Island. Captain Kidd was a privateer and pirate in the late 1600s. In 1699, he sailed from the Caribbean to Boston, where he was arrested for piracy. Kidd buried treasure on his way to Boston, including a sizeable loot on New York's Gardiner Island, some of which has been recovered. According to legend, Kidd also made a stop on Hog Island, where he stashed some of his treasure.

After his capture, Kidd was sent to England to stand trial for piracy and murder. The court found him guilty and hanged him. It took two tries to execute Kidd. The rope broke and Kidd survived his first hanging. Many folks in attendance at Kidd's execution believed this to be a sign from God

Captain Kidd hanging in chains.

Captain Kidd's body was hanged from chains and left on display as a warning to pirates. *Library of Congress.*

and demanded his release. However, the authorities did not relent and hanged Kidd again. This time, the rope held, and Kidd died. After his death, Kidd's body was hanged from chains over the River Thames to warn anyone thinking of becoming a pirate.

Whether or not Captain Kidd actually left treasure on Hog Island is debatable. It could be that his fame as a pirate started the tales. But even if Kidd did not a stash a loot on Hog Island, it is still possible that treasure is hidden on the island. In 1798, the *Inclination* was en route to Baltimore from Germany when it sank off Hog Island. According to some accounts, there were eighteen chests full of gold and silver coins aboard the vessel.

The treasure on Hog Island may not come from a shipwreck or a legendary pirate. It might have a more mundane explanation in the form of a well-known cheapskate. According to an article titled "History of Hog Island, VA," there was a man who lived on Hog Island named Samuel Kelly, whom folks called "the miser." He must have been tight with his money, because the article said, "There never lived a more thorough miser. He visited nobody, never entered a church, never gave a cent to charity, never had a decent coat on his back in all his life, and probably never sat down to a well-prepared meal." Kelly even spent his life living in a shabby, dilapidated cabin.

As a boy, Kelly "showed a decided bent for making money, and keeping it also. When he reached manhood he united the characteristics of Daniel Dancer, the miser, and that of the famous Captain Kidd; for he hoarded his money, and then buried it."

Kelly opened a store on the island—the only store—and took orders each day from the locals and delivered their goods in the evening. He made a good living doing it, but he did not endear himself to his neighbors. They became suspicious about his fortune: "There must be a fortune hid away somewhere in his cabin, for some of his neighbors had caught a passing glimpse through the window of the miser gloating over a great pile of gold coin."

As the years turned into decades, Kelly amassed more and more money and kept it all to himself. He died a lonely old man. "History of Hog Island, VA" said this about Kelly's last days:

> On his deathbed his friends and only surviving relative besought him to reveal the secret of the hiding place; but the ruling passion was strong in death. Shrouds have no pockets, but if the miser could not carry his treasure with him, no one else should, and soon he died carrying his secret to the grave. The house was searched, and under the counter in his little store was found two boxes, one containing three thousand dollars in gold, the other, two thousand in currency. Then a thorough hunt was organized and every possible or likely spot was examined but not another cent was ever discovered. His only relative and heir was his sister, ninety-four years of age.
>
> As the sands of Neversink keep secure the ill-gotten gains of Captain Kidd, so the shoals and sand of Hog Island hide from mortal eyes the thousands and thousands of dollars hidden away by Sam Kelly, the miser.

Captain Kirk's Treasure

No—not that Captain Kirk—not the commander of the starship *Enterprise*. Instead, this Captain Kirk was a pirate who buried his treasure in Fauquier County. As the story goes, Scottish-born William Kirk was thought to be a pirate who, between his outings, buried treasure on a tract of land formerly known as Snow Hill Farm in Fauquier County. (A housing subdivision now occupies the land.) Kirk died in 1779, but before he met his maker, he buried $60,000 worth of silver and gold coins; this would be worth more than $1.2 million today. As previously stated, silver and gold have outpaced the rate of inflation, so $1.2 million is a conservative estimate.

According to a 1984 *Washington Post* article, a century after Kirk buried his treasure, a tenant on the farm made a discovery while plowing a field. He unearthed gold coins known as "English guineas" and Spanish silver dollars called "pieces of eight" because each coin was worth eight Spanish reales. Weeks later, the tenant bought his own piece of land nearby for a price of $8,000. The *Washington Post* said, "It is thought the tenant spent all of what he found; the rest remains hidden."

These are but a few tales of pirate treasure in the commonwealth. There could be an inconceivable amount of pirate treasure buried in Virginia, but as Blackbeard said, only the devil knows where it is hidden.

Chapter 10

CONFEDERATE GOLD

There are not billions of dollars out there in lost treasures waiting to be reclaimed.
There are trillions of dollars of treasure waiting to be reclaimed.
—J. Hutton Pulitzer, 10 Treasure Legends!: Virginia

Mosby's Gold

There is no shortage of Civil War treasure legends in Virginia. One of my favorites is the tale of Mosby's gold. During the Civil War, Colonel John Singleton Mosby, nicknamed the "Gray Ghost," commanded the legendary Forty-Third Virginia Cavalry Battalion, a unit composed of irregular troops, or partisan rangers. Nicknamed Mosby's Rangers, these guerrilla fighters earned the scorn of the Union army with their swift and daring raids behind enemy lines. In the South, they became legends. General Robert E. Lee often criticized Mosby and the use of irregular troops, but nonetheless, he praised Mosby and said he was "zealous, bold, and skillful, and with very small resources he has accomplished a great deal."

Arguably, Mosby's most daring exploit was the capture of Union general Edwin Stoughton in present-day downtown Fairfax. After hosting a party, General Stoughton was sound asleep in his quarters on the night of March 9, 1863. He was in for the rudest of awakenings. According to Mosby's memoirs:

> *There was no time for ceremony, so I drew up the bedclothes, pulled up the*
> *general's shirt, and gave him a spank on his bare back, and told him to*

get up. As his staff officer was standing by me, Stoughton did not realize the situation and thought that somebody was taking a rude familiarity with him. He asked in an indignant tone what all this meant. I told him that he was a prisoner, and that he must get up quickly and dress. I then asked him if he had ever heard of "Mosby," and he said he had. "I am Mosby," I said. "Stuart's cavalry has possession of the Court House; be quick and dress."

In recent years, it has become taboo to praise the gallantry of Confederate officers such as Mosby, Stonewall Jackson, Turner Ashby and others. Be that as it may, you have to admit: it took some cojones to wake an enemy general with a smack on the butt in the middle of the night!

Not only did Mosby's Rangers make off with a Union general after their Fairfax raid, but they also nabbed thirty-two prisoners and fifty-eight horses. It was the loss of the horses that bothered President Lincoln when he learned of General Stoughton's capture. Lincoln said, "I did not mind the loss of the brigadier as much as I did the loss of the horses. For, I can make a much better brigadier in five minutes, but the horses cost a hundred and twenty-five dollars apiece."

Mosby turned over the prisoners and horses to General J.E.B. Stuart in Culpeper. But according to legend, he made a stop along the way. As the story goes, Mosby left Fairfax with a burlap sack filled with $350,000 worth of coins, jewelry and family heirlooms that Union forces had taken from Southern homes. Fearing an engagement with Union troops on his way to Culpeper, Mosby and his trusted sergeant James F. Ames buried the loot. The pair buried the treasure between two large pine trees "marked with an X." According to some accounts, the treasure is buried between New Baltimore and Warrenton; some say it lies in Fairfax County; others believe the cache is hidden somewhere between Warrenton and Culpeper; Haymarket also comes up, as well as a number of other possible locations.

As is so often the case with these legends, the stories are convoluted. Many retellings of the story claim Union troops captured Sergeant Ames and hanged him when he tried to retrieve the treasure. But this is not true. According to a historical marker (that I used to drive past every day on my commute) in Delaplane, Virginia: "On 9 Oct. 1864 a Federal soldier shot and killed Ames on the road leading to Benjamin 'Cook' Shacklett's house. The Union soldier was killed by Ranger Pvt. Ludwell Lake, Jr. Ames was buried nearby in an unmarked grave. Mosby said of Ames, 'I never had a more faithful follower.'"

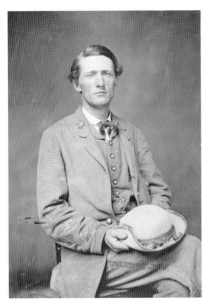

Left: Colonel John S. Mosby commanded the Forty-Third Battalion, Virginia Cavalry, a unit composed of partisan rangers. *Library of Congress.*

Right: This historical marker off U.S. 17 in Delaplane tells of the death of John Mosby's right-hand man. *Author's collection.*

So if this aspect of the story is untrue, how much of the rest can we believe? Mosby died in 1916 at the age of eighty-two. He had plenty of time to retrieve the loot and would have known exactly where to look. Why didn't he? But for me, that is where my skepticism ends. Though it would be easy to dismiss the story of Mosby's gold, if history has anything to tell us, it is that the Gray Ghost was not a man to underestimate. So maybe the cache is out there.

THE CONFEDERATE TREASURY

Virginia was arguably the most important Confederate state. It was the most populous, with over 1.5 million residents. Virginia was also the wealthiest state, thanks in large part to its industrial base. Virginia was the industrial hub of the Confederacy, and it equaled the output of all other Confederate states combined. As Virginia was the northernmost Confederate state and a state of such importance to the South's war effort, the majority of the Civil War was fought on its soil. The Civil War Sites Advisory Commission classified 384 Civil War engagements as "principal battles." Of those battles, 123 occurred in Virginia. Tennessee is a distant second with 38 principal battles.

When Virginia seceded from the Union, Richmond replaced Montgomery, Alabama, as the Confederate capital. The war made life in the capital miserable for residents. Food shortages, the lack of basic necessities and skyrocketing prices stirred resentment among the women of the city. While their husbands, brothers and fathers were on the battlefield, women and children had to fend for themselves in a climate of wartime scarcity. Feeling abandoned by the Confederate government, the women of Richmond took matters into their own hands. On April 2, 1863, Mary Jackson led three hundred armed women through the streets of Richmond. After Governor John Letcher refused to meet with the women and address their grievances, they looted stores and warehouses throughout the city. Local militia put down the uprising, and authorities arrested over sixty rioters.

Life in Richmond did not get any easier. The Union attempted to capture the capital on several occasions, but the city remained in Confederate hands until April 2, 1865. A day earlier, after a nine-month siege of Petersburg, Union forces broke Confederate lines. With this, General Robert E. Lee

Frank Leslie's Illustrated Newspaper ran a report on the Richmond Bread Riot. *Library of Congress.*

Richmond lay in ruins after its fall. *National Archives.*

decided to abandon Petersburg, Richmond's last line of defense. Lee's retreat ceded the Confederate capital to the Federal army. On Sunday morning, April 2, 1865, Lee sent a telegram to President Jefferson Davis. Davis read the message during a morning church service. It said: "I advise that all preparation be made for leaving Richmond tonight."

Chaos and turmoil ensued. Retreating Confederate soldiers burned the arsenal, supply warehouses, bridges and anything of value to the approaching Union army. The fires raged out of control and destroyed much of the city. Ragged, hungry citizens took to the streets. The *New York Times* reported:

> *At sunrise on Monday morning Richmond presented a spectacle that we hope never to witness again. The last of the Confederate officials had gone; the air was lurid with the smoke and flame of hundreds of houses weltering in a sea of fire.*
>
> *The streets were crowded with furniture and every description of wares, dashed down to be trampled in the mud or burned up where it lay. All the government storehouses were thrown open, and what could not be gotten off by the government was left to the people, who, everywhere ahead of the flames, rushed in, and secured immense amounts of bacon, clothing, boots, &c.*

One would expect mayhem to unfold as a city falls to its enemy. But the scene in Richmond turned ugly even by wartime standards. In a disgraceful act mocking the Southern honor culture, drunken Confederate deserters pillaged the city they had vowed to defend. The *New York Times* wrote:

When it was made known on Sunday morning that the evacuation of Richmond was a foregone conclusion, the City Council held a meeting, and in secret session passed an order for the destruction of all the liquor in the city. Accordingly, about the hour of midnight the work commenced, under the direction of committees of citizens in all the wards. Hundreds of barrels of liquor were rolled into the streets, and the heads knocked in. The gutters ran with a liquor freshet, and the fumes filled and impregnated the air. Fine cases of bottled liquors were tossed into the street from third story windows, and wrecked into a thousand pieces. As the work progressed some straggling Confederate soldiers, retreating through the city, managed to get hold of a quantity of liquor. From that moment law and order ceased to exist; chaos came, and a Pandemonium reigned.

Drunk with vile liquor, the soldiers—said to belong to GAREY's cavalry—roamed from store to store on Main-street, followed by a reckless

A drawing of the fall of Richmond on the night of April 2, 1865. *Library of Congress.*

crowd, drunk as they. With the butts of their muskets they dashed in the plate glass of the store doors, and entering, made a wreck of everything with the celerity of magic. Jewelry stores, clothing stores, boot and hat stores, and confectionary stores were objects of special attraction to these pillagers, who, be it remembered, were not Federal soldiers, but Confederate stragglers.

As Richmond fell, Confederate leadership turned its attention to the treasury and to their own escape. Jefferson Davis and his cabinet fled Richmond on a train bound for Danville, Virginia. The next day, Danville became the new Confederate capital. It was a short-lived tenure, only lasting a week. When General Robert E. Lee surrendered to General Ulysses S. Grant at Appomattox Courthouse on April 9, for all intents and purposes, the war was over. Fearing punishment by the Federal government, Davis and his cabinet fled to Greensboro, North Carolina.

There was gold waiting in Greensboro. During the evacuation of Richmond, soldiers loaded "the last train out of the city" with gold, silver and other valuables. Money worth $450,000 from Richmond banks also made the trip. Davis had the treasure loaded onto wagons. A wagon train then followed Davis on a southward trek as he tried to avoid capture.

A drawing of the capture of Jefferson Davis in Georgia. According to some accounts, he dressed himself in women's clothing to try to avoid capture. *Library of Congress.*

Davis deposited the Richmond bank money in a vault in Washington, Georgia. He had used much of the Confederate treasury to finance his own escape and pay soldiers. Some think Davis may have also stashed a large amount of money, intending to use it after Confederate leadership regrouped. He would not get the chance. On May 10, 1865, Union troops apprehended Davis near Irwinville, Georgia. Davis had very little money on him, leaving historians to ponder what became of the Confederate treasury.

The Richmond bank money has become intertwined in the Confederate treasury lore because much of it went missing, too. According to Robert Scott Davis, writing for the *New Georgia Encyclopedia*:

> *The remaining funds from the Richmond banks were left in Washington, Georgia. A detachment of Union soldiers set out to divert this specie to a railhead in South Carolina, but on May 24, 1865, bandits in Georgia attacked the wagons, which had stopped for the night at or around the Chennault Plantation in Lincoln County. Of the cache, $251,029 was lost.*

Officials recovered roughly $111,000, leaving around $140,000 of the known Richmond bank money unaccounted for. But this, and the treasury money Jefferson Davis may have stashed away, is only the tip of the iceberg.

The Confederate government did not keep official records of the contents in its treasury. Most believe the treasury held at least $500,000 in gold and silver. Some estimate, however, that there might have been as much as $20,000,000 in the treasury. Many think all the gold and silver from the treasury did not make it onto the last train out of the city. According to rumors, $3,000,000 in gold bullion is buried along the James River a few miles south of Richmond. Legend also holds that someone made off with $10,000,000 in gold—money the British government had loaned the Confederacy. This treasure is in the ground somewhere east of Hopewell.

There could be a vast amount of Confederate gold west of Richmond. One legend states that Confederate soldiers obtained $350,000 during raids in Pennsylvania and Maryland. They buried it on the commonwealth's tallest mountain, Mount Rogers. Supposedly, $60,000 in gold coins is buried near Saltville. Rumors state another $4,000,000 in gold is stashed on a farm west of Lynchburg. If even a small fraction of the purported Confederate gold is out there, in today's dollars, the fortune would be immense.

Chapter 11

THE GOVERNMENT WANTS THE GOLD

Gold is money. Everything else is credit.
—*J.P. Morgan*

The company I worked for in the early 2000s sent me to the Detroit area for a weeklong software class. I met a guy in class named Brad who worked for a large Texas-based oil company. Brad was a personable fellow with a quick wit, and he seemed to be the type that played the role of class clown in his youth. He looked about fifty years old, wore thick bifocals and had a flat-top haircut that you could set your watch to. Brad was a big boy, too. He stood around six feet, six inches and was about as broad as he was tall. His hands were the size of tennis racquets. I couldn't help but think that I would hate to have to tangle with him. Brad lived in "Loosiana," as he called it, but grew up in northern Alabama. With the two of us being southern boys, we hit it off and would go out to lunch during class and dinner afterward while we were in Detroit.

"So, you're from Virginia, you say?" Brad asked while we were out one evening.

"Yeah, born and raised," I replied.

"You're from where all that gold is, then."

"Gold?"

"Yeah, gold. There's gold all over Virginia. Old mines, gold veins—tons of it."

Gold all over Virginia? How can that be? I had lived in Virginia all my life, and this is the first I was hearing of it.

"You sure about that?" I asked him.

"Yeah, boy! Positive," Brad shot back. "About all the coins the settlers made in colonial times was from gold outta Virginia."

"That a fact?"

"Uh huh. Supposed to be some big deposits in central Virginia, but them ole tree-hugging types are keeping y'all from getting it out."

"I had no idea."

"The big gold is in the national forest. On them eastern ridges of the national forest land is where most of it is."

"Really?"

"They'll let you pan for it in streams, but you can't dig."

"No kidding?"

"Yeah. Why do you think it's national forest?"

"What? Well—"

"Ah, lemme guess. You think it's because the government wants to protect trees and cute little furry animals. Is that it?"

"I hadn't really thought about it before. I guess I just figured it was to preserve land for future generations and save it from development."

"Future generations…development…boy…" Brad burst out in laughter and shook his head the way my dad did after I said something stupid. Once he composed himself, he looked me in the eye and began sharing his theory that is so crazy it makes sense.

"How much land does the federal government own in your state?" he asked. "What is it, like two million acres?"

"Thereabouts," I said. "Probably north of that."

"Well, that's a buncha land, boy. And Virginia and places in the East don't even have much federal land compared to out west. Hell, I think Nevada is 80 percent federal."

"Yeah, so?"

"There's a reason the government has so much land. It ain't for spotted owls, waterfowl habitat or some damn species of salamander nobody's ever heard of. And it sure as hell ain't to give you a place to go hunting and hiking. Those things are just a distraction from the real story."

"Okay, I'll bite. Go on."

Brad took a swig of his Crown and Coke. He leaned in toward me for dramatic effect and whispered, "It's collateral."

"Collateral? What the hell for? What do you mean collateral?"

"The country is in debt up to its eyeballs. How do you think our feckless leaders keep borrowing money?"

"The Federal Reserve prints it. Duh!"

"Shut, Federal Reserve…boy…there's nothing federal about it, and they sure as hell don't have any reserves. The Fed is a private entity."

"All right. Now what's that got to do with the price of corn?"

"The Fed keeps printing money so these worthless politicians can spend more than they haul in with taxes."

"What a stunning revelation. Shocking. You've uncovered the 'big secret' behind deficit spending. Congrats, man." I gave him an eyeroll and a slight headshake. "Everybody already knows this, Nostradamus."

"But think about it—me and you can't borrow more money than we make."

"Yeah, but we ain't the gangsters in Congress."

"I know it. But there's a way we could borrow more. If we had—"

"Collateral. Something the bank could take if we didn't pay up. Something like…land."

"Bingo! Now you're using your noggin. Boy, I knew you were smarter than you looked."

"I'm not the sharpest tack in the drawer, but I'll stick you if you ain't careful."

"Hehe. What I'm getting at, is there's gold, silver, uranium, copper, oil and gas and who knows what else on all this so-called protected federal land. And that's the collateral they use for the central bankers. It's not the land so much as what's underneath it."

I was blown away. As crazy as Brad sounded, he made too much sense for me to dismiss. In fact, his half-baked theory made so much sense it had to be true.

"Brad, this is the first I've heard of this," I said.

"I'm not surprised. How old are you, boy?" he asked.

"Twenty-nine."

"Yeah, well, I got a little over twenty years on you. You're young yet. Just pay attention as you get older. What you're going to find is you can't believe a word that comes from the news. Not one word—"

"Again with another groundbreaking observation! You're on a roll this evening, John the Revelator."

"But listen, I've got a point—"

"Yeah. On the top of your head."

"Dammit boy…"

Above: Gold mining is back in Virginia, but many Buckingham County residents are not happy about it. *Author's collection.*

Left: Are national forests and national parks hiding the government's collateral in plain sight? *Author's collection.*

"I'm just playing. Please finish your thought."

"Anyhow, if you can't trust the news to tell the truth about current events, what does that say about the history books?"

"Hmmm…"

"You can't trust the government, you can't believe the news and the history books are full of crap. So when an ole boy from Alabama tells you something off the wall, he might be right."

Sound logic, indeed.

Hoarding Gold

The older I get and the more I look at what is going on in the world, Brad's words ring ever truer. And as I think about the things he said, I can't help but wonder if the federal government controls places like Assateague Island because of its buried gold. Think about it—Assateague Island alone could hold an immense fortune. Perhaps the feds recovered the loot already and used it to fund some sort of black project. A project that my grandkids might learn about someday. Before you call me crazy, take a look at unclassified National Security Agency documents. The NSA took an interest in the legendary Beale Treasure that supposedly lies in Bedford County, Virginia. Some think the NSA recovered the Beale Treasure and used it to fund projects free from congressional oversight.

Fortunately, there is still plenty of lost treasure in Virginia out of the reach of the feds. For example, according to a 1984 *Washington Post* article, in 1911, someone buried a cache of treasure in Warrenton. The "Bureau of Engraving Treasure—$31,700 in paper and a set of $20 bill plates—was supposedly buried near a creek bed just north of Warrenton, off Route 211." Then in 1929, a farmer south of Hopewell buried three half-gallon fruit jars full of gold and silver coins on his property. Presumably, the stock market crash spooked him, and he thought the ground was the safest place to keep his money. A lot of Depression-era folks did not trust banks and hid their money in all sorts of creative ways. At any rate, the farmer who buried the money died in an accident, and his jars full of coins remain hidden to this day.

I think it was smart of the farmer to bury his gold coins in 1929. This is why: in 1933, President Franklin Roosevelt signed Executive Order 6102 into law. Roosevelt blamed much of the nation's economic woes on "the hoarding of gold." Roosevelt's controversial executive order prohibited "the hoarding of gold coin, gold bullion, and gold certificates within the continental United States by individuals, partnerships, associations and corporations." The term "hoarding" meant owning more than $100 in gold. Section 2 of the Executive Order 6102 stated:

> *All persons are hereby required to deliver on or before May 1, 1933, to a Federal Reserve Bank or a branch or agency thereof or to any member bank of the Federal Reserve System all gold coin, gold bullion and gold certificates now owned by them or coming into their ownership on or before April 28, 1933, except the following:*
>
> *(a) Such amount of gold as may be required for legitimate and customary use in industry, profession or art within a reasonable time, including gold prior to refining and stocks of gold in reasonable amounts for the usual trade requirements of owners mining and refining such gold.*
>
> *(b) Gold coin and gold certificates in an amount not exceeding in the aggregate $100 belonging to any one person; and gold coins having a recognized special value to collectors of rare and unusual coins.*

Executive Order 6102 outlawed the private ownership of gold. *U.S. Government Printing Office.*

Those who turned in their gold received paper currency in the amount of $20.67 per troy ounce. Those who did not turn in their gold faced stiff penalties if caught. Section 9 laid out the consequences:

> *Whoever willfully violates any provision of this Executive Order or of these regulations or of any rule, regulation or license issued thereunder may be fined not more than $10,000, or, if a natural person, may be imprisoned for not more than ten years, or both; and any officer, director, or agent of any corporation who knowingly participates in any such violation may be punished by a like fine, imprisonment, or both.*

Outlawing the ownership of gold and confiscating the gold of the citizenry allowed the Federal Reserve to increase the money supply—a necessary step to fund Roosevelt's high-priced New Deal projects. Thankfully, President Gerald Ford repealed the executive order when he signed a bill legalizing the private ownership of gold. Today, the Federal Reserve is no longer bound by a gold standard and can simply print money out of thin air when the politicians demand it. As I write these words in 2022, inflation is at a forty-year high and still soaring. Many have started to question the wisdom of printing money on the whims of politicians. But as Brad said, as long as the federal government owns vast plots of land that hold gold and other commodities to secure their debts, the printing presses are sure to keep rolling.

PART III
WEIRD STORIES

Chapter 12

MYSTERY BOOMS

The first angel sounded his trumpet, and there came hail and fire mixed with blood, and it was hurled down on the earth. A third of the earth was burned up, a third of the trees were burned up, and all the green grass was burned up.
—Revelation 8:7 (New International Version)

In May 2011, the Associated Press reported, "A loud boom rattled Hampton Roads and the Eastern Shore but the source is a mystery." Some residents claimed the boom shook their houses and rattled their windows. There was no seismic activity in the area, according to the U.S. Geological Survey; a NASA spokesperson from Wallops Island said activity from the facility could not have caused the boom; and an Oceana Naval Air Station spokesperson said a sonic boom from the base could not travel as far as Suffolk. So what caused it?

Richmond CBS affiliate WTVR ran a story in 2014 about mysterious booms occurring across central Virginia. After the report, the station "received hundreds of tips....Some said the noises were so intense they rattled their homes." There was no explanation for the booms, but WTVR "determined the booms are not coming from Fort Lee or Fort Pickett. It was not the rock quarry in Dinwiddie or Chesterfield. Additionally, it was not a transformer explosion or a sonic boom."

On September 22, 2015, the mystery booms hit the Delmarva peninsula. Some thought military aircraft may have created sonic booms, but a spokesperson from Naval Air Station Patuxent River said, "We've received

NASA's Wallops Island facility denied responsibility for mysterious booms in the Chincoteague area. So what caused them? *Author's collection.*

a couple of calls regarding potential sonic booms felt last night around 8:30 and have researched our logs. We did not have any flights in that area last night." Officials at NASA Wallops Flight Facility and Dover Air Force Base also denied any involvement, and Chincoteague fire officials said there were no explosions on the island that could have caused the booms.

The *Bristol Herald Courier* reported on a rash of mystery booms that took place in 2017 across southwestern Virginia. Here, too, there were no obvious causes, and the booms remain a mystery.

These have been but a few examples from Virginia; the phenomenon is nationwide. In fact, as I pen these words in late March 2022, a couple of weeks ago, Houston, Texas, experienced a mystery boom. Although many believe an exploding meteor was to blame, no one has been able to positively identify the cause. About a month earlier, a mystery boom hit San Diego. This was on the heels of a rash of similar booms that occurred in Southern California throughout 2021.

It was not until 2013 that I started paying attention to reports of mystery booms. In fact, I did not know this was a phenomenon until I heard a guest discuss it on a late-night AM radio talk show. The guest gave details from cases all over the country in which strange booms had occurred, all without a known cause. From 2013 until now, it seems these strange occurrences have been taking place with far greater frequency and intensity.

Although most folks did not start paying attention to mystery booms until fairly recently—again, because of their increasing frequency and intensity—the phenomenon has been with us for an indeterminate amount of time. In 1997, the *Virginian-Pilot* ran a story about a mystery boom that residents from Norfolk to Suffolk heard; slight tremors accompanied the noise. However, it was not an earthquake that caused the tremors or noise. According to the article:

> *Dr. James Coble, associate professor of geology at Tidewater Community College, said the cause of the trembling probably was not an earthquake.*
>
> *"I looked at our seismograph here, and we have picked up something," he said. He said the cause was probably not a "natural" event. "It doesn't look like a tremor."*
>
> *Coble said the readings picked up on the machine could have been caused by a sonic boom, heavy construction work or military testing.*

Area military officials could not point to a cause for the event.

Going back further in time, Virginia-born Meriwether Lewis, best known for his role in the Lewis and Clark Expedition, wrote of mysterious noises in the Rocky Mountains. He called the sounds "unaccountable artillery," but undoubtedly, what he was hearing was the same thing as today's mystery booms. Lewis wrote that on June 13, 1805, he and his party

> *repeatedly witnessed a nois* [sic] *which proceeds from a direction a little to the N. of West as loud and resembling precisely the discharge of a piece of ordinance of 6 pounds at the distance of three miles. I was informed of it by the men several times before I paid any attention to it, thinking it was thunder most probably which they had mistaken. At length, walking in the plains the other day I heard this noise very distinctly. It was perfectly calm, clear, and not a cloud to be seen.*

Lewis said, "I am at a loss to account for this phenomenon." He is not alone. The funny thing about these mystery booms is that no one knows what causes them. Wikipedia calls mystery booms "skyquakes." Their entry for "skyquake" says, "The sound may cause noticeable vibration in a building or across a particular area. Those who experience skyquakes typically do not have a clear explanation for what caused them and they are perceived as 'mysterious.'" I could not help but notice the smug quotation marks around the word "mysterious"—as if only superstitious, uneducated folks would think of the phenomenon as a genuine mystery.

Explanations for mystery booms vary. The "experts" have proposed everything imaginable, including meteors causing sonic booms; sonic booms from military aircraft; the collapse of underwater caves; resonance

Meriwether Lewis of the Lewis and Clark Expedition was born in Ivy, Virginia, just west of Charlottesville. *Author's collection.*

from solar activity; volcanic eruptions; avalanches; "shallow" earthquakes that do not cause vibrations; and a host of other explanations.

By far, meteors are the favorite explanation for the phenomenon. Sonic booms from meteors were blamed for mystery booms in the Shenandoah Valley and Northern Virginia in 2021. But in these cases, observers spotted a fireball streaking across the sky. Oftentimes this is not the case, nor does anything appear on instruments indicating a meteor entered the atmosphere.

In February 2022, central and southside Virginia residents notified local authorities after hearing mystery booms. The sheriff's office in both Prince George County and Greensville County told concerned citizens there was nothing to worry about and the sounds were coming from Fort Pickett near Blackstone, Virginia. A spokesperson from Fort Pickett said the booms were from "live-fire training that frequently takes place," and it was "nothing out of the ordinary." On one hand, this makes sense. But then again, Fort Pickett is a good thirty miles from the Greensville County line. The Prince George County line is about forty miles away. This is a long way for the sound of artillery fire to travel and be loud enough to alarm residents. Even if, as the Fort Pickett spokesperson said, "atmospheric conditions can cause the sounds from the range to carry farther and sound louder than normal," it would seem folks living in the vicinity of a military installation would be used to live-fire exercises and would have heard them in all sorts of atmospheric conditions. Having worked at Marine Corps Base Quantico for a few years, I know that live-fire exercises took place regularly. But there was a noticeable difference between these and the hellacious noise from the 2011 "Virginia earthquake." The point being, it seems to me that maybe the sounds coming from Fort Pickett were not ordinary live-fire. Or maybe, live-fire did take place at the fort, but this was not the cause of the mystery booms.

Like most other strange phenomena, certain instances of mystery booms can be explained, but the phenomenon as a whole cannot be.

When the Trumpet Sounds

Since roughly 2005, folks have reported hearing the eerie sound of trumpets emanating from the sky. In 2015, the phenomenon began receiving widespread attention and reporting. In Virginia, reports of trumpets in the sky come from Virginia Beach, Prince William County, Gloucester County, southwestern Virginia and more. According to the *New York Post*, the *Guardian* and other news outlets, there was an uptick of trumpet sounds in 2020, especially from places affected by harsh COVID-19 lockdowns.

Much like the mystery booms occurring all over, there is no explanation for these "sky trumpets" either. Are the two connected? Could they be variations of the same phenomenon? Some call the strange noises the "sound of the apocalypse" after the Seven Trumpets in the Book of Revelation. Are the unexplained sounds a precursor to the doomsday predictions in the Bible?

In the Book of Revelation, Jesus Christ opens the "Seven Seals." When he opens the first six seals, some sort of calamity occurs on Earth. For instance, when he opens the first four seals, the "Four Horsemen of the Apocalypse" appear. The first horseman is the Antichrist, who rides a white horse; the second horseman rides a red horse and represents war; the third horseman sits atop a black horse and smites the earth with famine; the fourth horseman rides a pale horse and his name is Death—and Hell follows him.

When Christ opens the fifth seal, it releases the cries of the martyrs; they demand vengeance. The opening of the sixth seal unleashes earthquakes and natural disasters such as the world has never seen. The rulers of nations, the billionaire class and so-called elite of the world hide in caves alongside the poor and wish to die rather than face the "wrath of the Lamb."

The seventh seal is different; when Christ opens it, nothing happens. Silence falls on Heaven for half an hour. When the silence lifts, seven angels, each holding a trumpet, prepare to sound them. The sounding of the first trumpet burns a third of the planet. After the second trumpet, a "burning mountain"—probably an asteroid—falls to the sea, killing a third of marine

The 1887 painting *The Four Horsemen of the Apocalypse* by Victor Vasnetsov. *Wikimedia Commons.*

life and wiping out a third of the world's ships. When the third trumpet sounds, a falling star poisons a third of the freshwater sources on the planet. A third of the light from the sun, moon and stars goes dark when the fourth angel blows the trumpet.

The blowing of the next three trumpets unleashes things so horrible, the Bible calls them the "three woes." The fifth trumpet signals the angel of the abyss, Abaddon, to lead a swarm of locusts to torment humankind. These are no ordinary locusts; they sting like scorpions, and their sting is so painful that those afflicted "will long to die, but death will elude them." As a side note, author Hal Lindsey popularized the notion that the locusts are in reality military helicopters in his 1970 book *The Late Great Planet Earth.* According to Lindsey, John the Revelator described the helicopters in the only way he knew how, having never seen such advanced technology. Some believe Lindsey's theory birthed the popular "black helicopter" conspiracy theory. But more on that later.

The sixth trumpet releases four angels bound in chains. These angels command an army of 200 million, and they kill a third of the earth's population. Revelation 11:15 tells of the seventh trumpet: "The seventh angel sounded his trumpet, and there were loud voices in heaven, which said: 'The kingdom of the world has become the kingdom of our Lord and of his Messiah, and he will reign for ever and ever.'" (New International Version)

Since 2020, we have been facing a global pandemic. As 2021 came to a close, it literally rained fish in Texarkana, Texas. As I write these words, in March 2022, many feel we are on the brink of World War III with the Russian invasion of Ukraine. A couple of days ago, President Biden said the world would soon face food shortages. In Matthew 24:6–8, Jesus said:

> *6 And you will hear of wars and rumors of wars. See that you are not troubled; for all these things must come to pass, but the end is not yet. 7 For nation will rise against nation, and kingdom against kingdom. And there will be famines, pestilences, and earthquakes in various places. 8 All these are the beginning of sorrows. (New King James Version)*

Only the beginning of sorrows—how bad is it going to get? Are we doomed? Is the end near? Maybe. But then again, wars, hunger, disease and natural disasters have always been with us. Since the beginning of time, prophets have predicted the end of the world—yet here we are. Besides, the Book of Revelation can be interpreted in dozens of different ways, as can sky trumpets and mystery booms. They are not literally telling us we are on the brink of the apocalypse—right?

Chapter 13

GHOST LIGHTS AND UFOs

All phenomena are real in some sense, unreal in some sense, meaningless in some sense, real and meaningless in some sense, unreal and meaningless in some sense, and real and unreal and meaningless in some sense.
—*Robert Anton Wilson*

There is a strange phenomenon known as "ghost lights"—instances of anomalous lights that move in erratic patterns, appear and disappear and change colors. These mysterious lights do not have a known cause and appear at certain spots around the world. Two famous examples are the Brown Mountain Lights in North Carolina and the Marfa Mystery Lights in Texas. In both places, strange lights inexplicably appear and disappear in the night sky. The lights move in random patterns, change colors and simply defy logic. I have witnessed the lights in both of these locations. In 2021, I saw the Marfa Mystery Lights from a viewing platform about nine miles outside the town of Marfa. Shortly after dark, strange lights appeared on the desert horizon; they were as bright as the flash from an electric arc welding machine. The lights moved in an erratic manner, disappeared and reappeared later. I cannot explain what I saw that night. From an overlook off Highway 181, about an hour's drive from Asheville, North Carolina, I saw the famous Brown Mountain Lights in both 2018 and 2020. Here, white lights twinkled like stars before bursting into orange, red and yellow spheres that rapidly darted back and forth in all directions. The lights were amazing, and I felt privileged to see them.

Above: If you pick the right night, and if you are lucky, you might spot the famous Brown Mountain Lights from an overlook off Highway 181 near Linville, North Carolina. *Author's collection.*

Left: A plaque at the Marfa lights viewing platform about nine miles outside Marfa, Texas. *Author's collection.*

I came away from Marfa and Brown Mountain perplexed by some of the ridiculous rationalizations skeptics use to try and explain away the mystery lights. What I saw was not the product of "swamp gas"; I was not hallucinating; this was not ball lightning; these were not lights from automobiles, trains or aircraft; they were not fires or flashlights; and a host of other explanations do not fit either.

Virginia is not to be left out of the ghost light discussion. In the Great Dismal Swamp, witnesses commonly spot the sudden appearance of strange lights. Some blame the lights on the "Lady of the Lake," a Native American maiden who died on her wedding day. Some think she is the source of the lights as she paddles a white canoe across Lake Drummond. There are also mundane explanations such as "swamp gas"—methane gas from decomposing plants that can cause flashes of light. Skeptics love this explanation and use it to dismiss everything from strange lights to UFOs and even cryptid sightings. Some blame the lights in the Great Dismal Swamp on smoldering peat moss. Then there is foxfire—certain fungi present on decaying wood produce a bioluminescent glow called foxfire. But for all the explanations skeptics put forth, no one knows for sure what causes the strange lights in the Great Dismal Swamp.

The Ghost Light of Cohoke Crossing

It is not surprising that a place as eerie as the Great Dismal Swamp would host strange lights in the night sky. But the best example of ghost lights in Virginia comes from a railroad crossing in King William County. The Cohoke Crossing near West Point, which lies along Mount Olive–Cohoke Road, is world famous for its mysterious lights. I visited the spot in the late 1990s but did not have the same luck as I did at Marfa and Brown Mountain. I did not spot anything out of the ordinary, although I did have an eerie feeling. Perhaps the feeling was more a product of things I had read about the lights rather than something supernatural. So I have nothing to report from my visit. However, for over a century, others have spotted strange lights along the tracks. According to eyewitnesses, on certain nights, a yellowish light resembling a "swinging lantern" appears down the railroad tracks. Some claim the light is brilliant white and races down the tracks like an oncoming train, filling onlookers with a sudden rush of fear. The speeding light will often reverse course or just simply disappear. Some have claimed the light begins as a bright light—as bright as a welding arc—and suddenly bursts into multiple colored lights and then vanishes.

Some say the lights at Cohoke Crossing were far more active during the 1960s and 1970s than they are today. Back then, the lights were such an attraction that crowds from all over gathered along the railroad tracks at night hoping to catch a glimpse; some drove from as far away as Florida, New York and Pennsylvania. In those days, there were many instances of people shooting their guns down the tracks at the lights. Some believed that shooting made the lights more active.

There is no explanation for the Cohoke ghost light, but one legend states that it is a phantom train. According to the story, Union soldiers killed a train full of Confederate soldiers bound for West Point and destroyed the train. Today, the doomed train full of spectral soldiers still makes its way down the tracks from time to time. Another story tells of a brakeman who was decapitated in a fatal accident. The yellowish, swinging light folks see is the brakeman holding a lantern, searching for his head. Needless to say, neither of these stories seems likely. But then again, they are as good of an explanation for the phenomenon as anything else.

UFOs

On January 3, 2014, Washington, D.C. station WJLA ABC 7 reported a UFO sighting from Ashburn. The report included video footage of two bright lights moving in an erratic fashion. Chris Smith, who saw the lights, said, "You couldn't help but see it in the sky, it was that bright." Smith began recording the objects on his cell phone and called his children to come see them. "To watch lights move, drop and stop, change direction and go out, come in with just a smooth silent grace, it was strange," he said. Being so close to Dulles International Airport, I can almost hear the skeptics claim Smith saw a low-flying aircraft or a blimp or use some other cockamamie excuse. But nothing from the airport moves that way.

Since Smith's sighting, witnesses have spotted a slew of UFOs over Ashburn and reported them to the National UFO Reporting Center (NUFORC). A few days after Smith's sighting, a witness claimed:

> *Saw bright specular point of light following chemtrail. Got my binoculars and focused in. Thought it was jet not emitting trail. Common to see pairs up there, one emitting trail, the other not. Bright shiny metallic sphere, followed*

parallel along chemtrail and then stopped, Hovered, floated under chemtrail then reversed direction. Shrunk in size. Grew in size and reflected sunlight again as before. Then dimmed, turned gray, then QUICKLY SHRUNK TO DOT AND DISAPPEARED IN ABOUT 2 SECONDS!

Someone spotted a "highly reflective object over Ashburn, not [a] bird, balloon, [or] aircraft," on January 24, 2014. In 2015, a witness observed "more than 12 objects bunched together in the sky" while driving in Ashburn. The objects were disk-shaped with red, green and white lights. The witness said, "They came down quickly. It was almost like a sudden drop then they darted off in different directions." Perhaps these were drones, but that many drones together along a road seems unlikely.

In November 2015, NUFORC received a report in which a witness in Ashburn "saw a green light move at a steady rate of speed across half of the sky in approximately one and a half seconds." The object disappeared "approximately 20 degrees from the horizon."

A circular object with red lights hovered for about six minutes in Ashburn at around 3:00 a.m. on May 14, 2016. A round object made a "loud whooshing sound" as it passed over a house in Ashburn on June 24, 2017. According to the report, the object left a trail and changed color. The witness's pets reacted to the object.

In November 2016, a witness saw a cluster of blue orbs while driving to his home in Ashburn. The witness's radio began malfunctioning when they appeared. The orbs were "blue that is akin to the color of dark tropical water." The majority of the orbs "clustered in a vertical line and to the immediate right around five of these orbs were spread out but still within the height of the first vertical cluster." When the witness got home, the orbs were still visible, but they eventually disappeared.

A cylindrical object landed in Ashburn on November 15, 2020. A man and his wife first noticed the object from their window; it was hovering in midair. The object then moved down the street, where it stayed in place over a soccer field. The object started moving straight down as if it were landing and then "appeared to morph into a car." The craft "evaporated or disappeared on landing and was never there after touching down."

In May 2021, a witness reported six to eight lights "equal in brightness to the stars." According to the report on the NUFORC database:

The lights were steady and did not blink like the normal air traffic in the area. They were observed southwest of Ashburn, VA. They were equidistant from each other and appeared to move in a circular pattern from west to the south. As they continued south they were no longer visible. They moved at a moderate speed similar to that of an airplane keeping equal space from each other the whole time.

Keep in mind these are only reports that I pulled from the NUFORC online database. There are several other well-known databases where witnesses also submit reports of their UFO sightings. Also, these are only reports that occurred in Ashburn from 2014 to 2021. I did not include sightings from nearby towns such as Leesburg, Sterling, Purcellville, Chantilly and Manassas—there are scores of sightings from these places, too. I left out three reports, two of which I think can be explained by drones and one was probably a Starlink satellite.

On February 22, 2020, my wife and I spotted two UFOs in Clarke County, about thirty minutes from Ashburn. We were driving to our home in Stephens City, Virginia, from Leesburg at around 10:00 p.m. and noticed two brilliant white spheres shortly after we crossed the Shenandoah River on Route 7. Both spheres moved in rapid, weird side-to-side and up-and-down motions. They seemed to fly at an altitude that we had seen military and police helicopters fly in the area before. As we drove along, the object on the left slowly dimmed. It grew dimmer and dimmer until we could no longer see it. After it disappeared, the other sphere thrust straight up into the sky and quickly took off to the northwest. Within seconds, we lost sight of it. Then, the object that had dimmed and disappeared burst into a blinding orange color and started moving south. We lost it in the trees as it was flying even lower and faster than before. After turning south onto U.S. 340, we saw the object again after passing through the town of Berryville. By now, the sphere had gained altitude; it had turned yellow and was not as bright. The object moved in an erratic pattern and headed west in the direction of Interstate 81. Shortly before we reached White Post, the object disappeared from our view. During the encounter, my wife tried in vain to record the spheres, but they were too far away, it was too dark and her phone was unable to capture anything of value.

I had another UFO sighting about seven months earlier. This occurred on July 13, 2019, at around 11:00 p.m. I do not remember why, but I was standing in the driveway of my home in Stephens City when I suddenly noticed an object brighter than any star I had ever seen. It was moving in an erratic, rapid side-to-side motion. I called out to my wife to come and see it, and we watched it for a couple of minutes. Whatever it was climbed straight up and quickly darted back down. It then held itself in place for about a minute. While in place, the object randomly shook and pulsated for a few seconds at a time. When it resumed its movements, it burst toward the east. It then climbed in a northeasterly direction until it disappeared from my view. My wife and I both took videos with our phones, but our videos are worthless. We could not get our camera phones to focus against the dark sky.

Probably unrelated, the same night as my Stephens City UFO sighting, a witness in Centreville reported, "A dot in the night sky directly above, too large to be a star caught my attention and then it moved (fast), paused, and disappeared."

With just the handful of recent, localized UFO sightings I have highlighted, it should be obvious that the UFO phenomenon is widespread. It also does not discriminate. Men and women, people of all ethnicities, blue-collar and white-collar workers and people of varying education levels—basically, folks from all walks of life—spot these strange lights and objects in the sky. What are they?

Chapter 14

THE WITCH OF PUNGO

Everyone loves a witch hunt as long as it's someone else's witch being hunted.
——*Walter Kirn*

When thinking of the witch hunts and witch trials of America's colonial days, it is undoubtedly Salem, Massachusetts, that comes to mind first. But an irrational fear of witches gripped many of the colonies and even touched Virginia. However, to the credit of the citizens of Virginia, the mass hysteria of New England did not make its way south. Moreover, there are no records that indicate Virginia executed any so-called witches. Authorities in Virginia had little interest in pursuing allegations of witchcraft, and the courts were not quick to hear such cases. In fact, in Virginia, when a court acquitted a defendant charged with witchcraft, the accused had the right to sue their accusers for slander. Most did. That said, the occasional witch trial did take place in the Old Dominion, especially in the seventeenth century.

The earliest recorded witchcraft case in Virginia goes back to September 1622, when a jury heard the case against Goodwife Joan Wright. Wright came under fire for allegedly predicting three deaths and causing an illness that afflicted several others. There is no record of the outcome of the case. This was common for the day. Known records show nineteen witch trials took place in Virginia during the seventeenth century. The overwhelming majority of the trials resulted in acquittals. There were a handful of witchcraft cases in the eighteenth century, and Virginia's last witch trial took place in 1802.

The most famous witch trial in Virginia occurred in July 1706. This was the trial of Grace White Sherwood, better known as the "Witch of Pungo." Before her famous trial, Sherwood had been accused of witchcraft several times. In 1697, Richard Capps claimed Sherwood used a spell to kill one of his bulls. The court failed to convict Sherwood. After the trial, Sherwood sued Capps for defamation and received a settlement. Sherwood faced two allegations of witchcraft in 1698. John and Jane Gisburne claimed Sherwood "was a witch and bewitched their pigs to death and bewitched their cotton." Elizabeth Barnes claimed that Sherwood came to her home one night and whipped "her and went out of the keyhole or crack of the door like a black cat." Local authorities failed to convict Sherwood of either charge. She then took legal action against her accusers for slander, but the court found in favor of the defendants.

Elizabeth Hill brought witchcraft charges against Sherwood in 1706. She accused Sherwood of bewitching her, causing her to have a miscarriage. Princess Anne County (now part of Virginia Beach) judges assembled two female jury panels to investigate. They tasked the first panel with searching Sherwood's home for suspicious imagery. The second panel had the job of examining Sherwood's body for "demon suckling teats." To their credit, both juries refused to appear.

On July 10, 1706, local authorities subjected Sherwood to "ducking" to determine whether she was a witch. Ducking was a process in which officers of the court tied a suspected witch's hands and feet and threw her into the water. The thought behind the procedure was that water is pure; it would regurgitate an evil witch and cause her to float. One not guilty of witchcraft would sink. Generally speaking, care was taken so that the accused would not drown in their trial by water, but obviously, the practice was dangerous and could turn into a no-win situation for the accused.

The authorities took Sherwood to the plantation of John Harper, which lay alongside the Lynnhaven River, for her ducking. A group of women examined her body to make sure she did not have any objects in her possession to free herself. The sheriff bound Sherwood in the "customary manner"—right thumb tied to the left big toe and left thumb tied to the right big toe. After the sheriff and a magistrate had rowed about two hundred yards from shore, they threw her into the water. The years of allegations finally caught up to Grace Sherwood; in her watery trial, she floated. To make matters worse, when she came ashore, a group of women onlookers discovered the "Devil's markings" on her body. Court records state that "five ancient women" swore under oath that Sherwood was not like other women and that she had "two things like tits

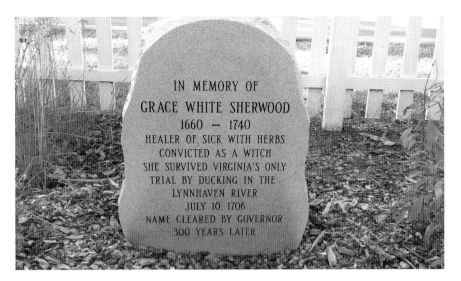

A memorial for Grace Sherwood at the herb garden at Old Donation Episcopal Church in Virginia Beach. *Wikimedia Commons.*

on her private parts of a black color." This was enough to convict Sherwood and send her to jail pending further proceedings. From here, the official records run out, and it is not clear what occurred in the aftermath. Most think Sherwood spent nearly eight years in jail.

Sherwood died in 1740 at the age of eighty. She lies in an unmarked grave near the intersection of Princess Anne Road and Old Pungo Ferry Road in Virginia Beach. Even in death, Sherwood could not escape rumors of witchcraft. According to *The Beach: A History of Virginia Beach, Virginia*:

> *As she lay ill during a fierce storm, Grace asked one of her sons to move her from her bed and place her feet into the warm ashes of the fireplace. During the night a tremendous gust of wind came down the chimney, scattering embers everywhere. When Grace's sons looked in on her, they discovered she had disappeared. All that remained of their mother was the imprint of a cloven hoof in the ashes.*

On the 300th anniversary of Grace Sherwood's ducking, the Commonwealth of Virginia cleared her of wrongdoing. Governor Tim Kaine issued an informal pardon to "officially restore the good name of Grace Sherwood." Legend holds that during July each year, observers witness strange lights above Witch Duck Bay. Many think the lights are a supernatural manifestation commemorating the ducking of Grace Sherwood.

Chapter 15

GHOST TOWNS AND FAKE TOWNS

We are addresses in ghost towns. We are old wishes that never came true.
—*Pete Wentz*

In a previous chapter, I mentioned the rumors of buried treasure on Hog Island, one of Virginia's barrier islands. Like most of the barrier islands that help protect the Virginia coastline from storms, Hog Island is unpopulated. But this was not always the case. Since colonial times, people lived on Hog Island, and it once held a thriving town named Broadwater. According to *History of Hog Island, VA*, at the turn of the twentieth century:

> *There are, all told, forty-two dwellings on the island, and every householder is well-to-do. Every year the island exports 150,000 bushels of oysters, the average price being fifty cents a bushel. The fish and game bring as much more; and aside from this, the life-saving station and lighthouse employees receive liberal wages; making the income of each householder fully $750 per annum. And this amount is never spent. In this community there is not a man who is in debt.*

Fierce storms regularly batter the Virginia barrier islands; understandably, life on narrow, low-lying Hog Island was precarious at best. In the mid- to late 1800s, rapid beach erosion forced the construction of a new lighthouse on the island. Hurricanes hammered Hog Island in the late 1800s, and in 1903, a devastating hurricane flooded the entire island. According to *History of Hog Island, VA*:

On October 10, 1903, Hog Island had an experience that has never occurred since the sea cast it up from the bowels of the deep. Tradition tells of high tides, and tidal waves like the one in 1888, which engulfed Cobb's Island but a few miles away; but never before has the whole of Hog Island disappeared from view as it did in October, leaving not one inch of natural land visible.

In 1933, the island flooded again during a hurricane, and life became untenable for residents. By the 1940s, the last of the islanders had abandoned their homes and headed for the mainland. They loaded many of the houses and buildings in Broadwater on barges and relocated them to the towns of Oyster and Willis Wharf on the Eastern Shore. Broadwater was no more, and today, it is a dim memory. After three hundred years of habitation, all that remains on Hog Island is a breed of feral sheep descended from those brought there in the seventeenth century.

West of South Hill, the decaying remains of the town of Union Level tell the story of brighter days. At one time, Union Level was a popular stop for travelers using horse-drawn carriages. The town flourished when the Southern Railroad replaced the old carriage lines. However, after the Civil War, Union Level started to falter. According to an article by Hilda Thompson, who grew up in Union Level:

Landowners would not sell property for tobacco warehouses, forcing tobacco sellers to establish their market in South Hill. Efforts to purchase land in Union Level for other businesses, including a textile mill and even a funeral home, were similarly futile. The bank and several other businesses closed in the wake of the Depression of 1929 and the 1930's. The drug store and two general merchandise stores closed in the 1970's. The train stopped running through Union Level by the mid-1980's and the depot was torn down. The U.S. Postal Service closed the post office in the 1990's.... With the decline of the railroad, the switch to supermarkets as a result of automobiles and improved roads, and the decline in small family farming profits, there is no railroad and no operating stores, post office, local school or business establishments in Union Level today.

Today, abandoned storefronts line a country road, reminding passersby that the good times packed up and left Union Level long ago.

A farming town in Cumberland County named Ca Ira once thrived and held much promise. According to the Cumberland County Historical Society, in 1836:

The village of Ca Ira contained approximately 40 dwellings, three mercantile stores, a merchant mill, a tobacco warehouse, two taverns, a non-denominational church, and a masonic hall. The population at the time was 310....Amongst the residents were two blacksmiths, two wheelwrights, two tailors and two plough manufacturers.

Ca Ira fell into decline in the aftermath of the Civil War, and by the early 1900s, not much was left of the town. Today, a church and "five modest dwellings" are all that remain. Were it not for the internet and road trippers, Ca Ira might have been forgotten altogether.

In the early days of the nation, founders such as George Washington dreamed of a series of canals that would allow for the transportation of goods throughout the country and open the lands in the West. In Fairfax County, a set of rapids and waterfalls known as Great Falls was an obstacle to crossing the Potomac River. A canal was necessary to circumvent this section of river. After the Virginia legislature issued a charter, the town of Matildaville sprang up, and construction began on a canal. Matildaville served as the headquarters of the Patowmack Company from 1785 to 1799. However, low water levels made the canal a failure, and today, all that is left of Matildaville are scattered ruins along a hiking trail in Great Falls Park.

Aside from Hog Island, I have visited all of these places. They are lonely and forgotten. I always get a little sad when I see places like this. Thinking of better days, prosperous times and dreams that did not come true for the people who used to live in these towns leaves me with a heavy feeling. The British explorer Percy Fawcett said it best in his book *Exploration Fawcett: Journey to the Lost City of Z*:

There is something ineffably sad about a ghost town. Imagination pictures the everyday life of the vanished people—their joys and sorrows, their aspirations and pastimes. When human beings abandon a dwelling they inevitably leave behind some shreds of their own personalities; and a deserted city has a melancholy so powerful that the least sensitive visitor is impressed by it.

Towns come and go; promising businesses and industries burn white hot and inevitably fizzle out. For every boom cycle, there is a bust cycle lurking around the corner. Weather and wars force people to leave their places of residence. New roads closed factories and abandoned railways kill off struggling towns. In my travels, I have seen towns on the brink of collapse all over the country. Although it is sad to see, this is the natural order of things. But in Virginia, along with the scattered ghost towns across the state, there are a couple of towns meant to be empty—fake towns.

Fake Towns

Just east of Richmond in Henrico County lies the 2,200-acre Elko Tract. The federal government commandeered the land for Elko Tract during World War II and set up a decoy city. It was a genius plan. Should the Japanese or Germans enter Virginia airspace with the intent of unleashing a bombing raid, our military had a plan divert them—our enemies would mistakenly bomb Elko Tract instead of Richmond. Elko Tract had an airfield similar to the airfield in Richmond, and its streets, lights and buildings were laid out in a similar manner. If and when the time came, the plan was to kill the lights in Richmond through a rolling blackout and turn on the lights at Elko Tract. Of course, neither the Nazis nor the Imperial Japanese threatened Virginia's capital, but the plan for Elko Tract was brilliant, nonetheless.

After the war, the federal government transferred ownership of Elko Tract to the Commonwealth of Virginia. The state planned to build "a mental institution/state hospital for African Americans" (Virginia was a segregated society at the time), but funding issues put a halt to construction. Some think by the 1960s, the federal government had purchased Elko Tract back from the Commonwealth of Virginia. It was around this time that rumors of shadowy activity at Elko Tract spread throughout the area. Some think one of our three-letter agencies might have used Elko Tract for training purposes. Others suggest it may have served as a Cold War relocation site—a site outside Washington, D.C., where government functions would carry on in the aftermath of a Soviet attack on our nation's capital. Today, the land is privately owned and completely off limits.

This historic marker tells of the decoy airfield at Elko Tract. *Courtesy of Abandoned Country.*

There are other fake towns used by our intelligence agencies. "The Farm" inside Camp Peary in Williamsburg is home to "a simulated *Truman Show* set in a fictionalized country called the Republic of Vertania." Here, CIA agents "undergo the most demanding espionage training on Earth." With the aid of Hollywood stage designers, the FBI set up a fake town at its training academy in Quantico. Named Hogan's Alley, the fake town holds a laundromat, bank, post office, barbershop, houses, stores and more. FBI agents and their partners perform training exercises in this pretend town—a town that resembles main street America in every way.

These are just a few fake towns that we know of. What don't we know? Maybe some of the small towns we drive through—those places where something "just doesn't feel right" but you cannot put your finger on why— have been set up to hide clandestine operations in plain sight. Who can say? And with the small number of forgotten ghost towns mentioned in this chapter, it is fair to wonder—how many other towns came and went that we have no record of? Do we really know our history, and can we be sure of what is taking place in the world around us?

Chapter 16

A GOOD CONSPIRACY
IS AN UNPROVABLE ONE

I'm telling you the government is up to some wicked stuff.
Of course, they've been at it for over a century now, so…
—*Angela Mullins,* Working for Uncle Henry

Dinosaurs never existed.
Epstein did not kill himself.
There was a second shooter on the grassy knoll.
The earth is flat.

The *Titanic* did not hit an iceberg—J.P. Morgan had it sunk to eliminate powerful individuals opposed to the creation of the Federal Reserve.

The moon landings are fake; Stanley Kubrick helped NASA film them in a studio. Actually, space is fake.

Princess Diana was murdered.

Elvis faked his death to hide from the Mafia.

Global elites are hell-bent on creating the "New World Order"—a totalitarian one-world government.

Those are but a few popular conspiracy theories; there are hundreds of others. I have always been fascinated by these outlandish claims. I believe some conspiracy theories are true; I am on the fence with others; and I dismiss many outright. But no matter how crazy a conspiracy theory sounds, I will usually at least hear it out. One of the wackier conspiracy theories involves a popular soft drink. For those old enough to remember New Coke, the godawful soft drink released in 1985, the theory purports that Coca-Cola executives

In a 1990 speech, President George H.W. Bush said, "Now, we can see a new world coming into view. A world in which there is the genuine prospect of new world order." *Library of Congress.*

Some called the Georgia Guidestones in Elbert County, Georgia, the Ten Commandments of the New World Order. Inscriptions such as "maintain humanity under 500,000,000 in perpetual balance with nature" fanned the flames of conspiracy. A mysterious explosion destroyed the monument in July 2022. *Author's collection.*

might have had duplicitous motives behind its introduction. Some think, me included, that the New Coke scheme was cover for the Coca-Cola Company to reintroduce the "original" formula now called Coca-Cola Classic. Except this formula was not the original—instead, it incorporated inferior, cheaper ingredients. I don't care what anybody says: Coke has not tasted quite the same since greedy executives orchestrated their devious New Coke conspiracy.

Of course, any conspiracy worth its salt cannot be proven. Mel Gibson's character, Jerry Fletcher, says it best in the 1997 film *Conspiracy Theory* when Alice Sutton, played by Julia Roberts, asks Jerry if he has proof of the crazy conspiracy theories he is throwing around. Jerry responds, "Absolutely not. I mean, a good conspiracy is an unprovable one." Indeed.

MATTRESS STORES, BLACK HELICOPTERS AND WEATHER CONTROL

So-called conspiracy theorists have shouted from the rooftops for decades that the weather is being manipulated. Nowadays, we know this is a fact—at least to a degree. The National Oceanic and Atmospheric Administration says the following on its website:

> *In the late 1940's and 1950's many deemed "the deliberate or the inadvertent alteration of atmospheric conditions by human activity," also known as weather modification, as a promising science of the future. Currently, the most common form of weather modification is cloud seeding, which increases rain or snow, usually for the purpose of increasing the local water supply. Weather modification can also have the goal of preventing damaging weather, such as hail or hurricanes, from occurring.*

The government and their lackeys in the corporate media use terms such as "benign weather modification" to act as though cloud seeding and other weather modification practices are not a big deal. Maybe I'm nuts, but the weather seems to be getting worse instead of better—much worse. I do not have statistics to back it up, but having lived my entire life in Virginia, it was not until the mid- to late 1990s that I remember experiencing my first tornado warning. Nowadays, even west of the Blue Ridge, tornado watches and warnings are just part of the weather in the spring, summer and early fall. So what are they *really* doing to the weather? What is going on beyond what they have admitted to?

The government is a lot like a lying ex-girlfriend, ex-boyfriend or ex-spouse: it will confirm many of your suspicions. When pressed, it will even admit to wrongdoing. But the whole truth is always far worse than you imagined in the first place.

You used to hear a lot about unmarked black helicopters in conspiracy theory circles. But they have sort of gone the way of the Bermuda Triangle, acid rain and quicksand—nobody talks much about them anymore. In the 1990s and early 2000s, there were scores of black helicopter sightings across central Virginia. I suspect they are still out there flying around, but they do not seem to alarm folks the way they used to. When I finally spotted one of the fabled matte black helicopters outside Bowling Green, Kentucky, in 2020, all I could think was how I wished to have seen it twenty years earlier. Back then, they were all the rage on late-night AM talk radio.

Since the 1970s, reports of unmarked black helicopters have come from all over the country. There have even been sightings from as far away as the United Kingdom. The mysterious helicopters show up in the vicinity of UFO sightings and cattle mutilations. They are also associated with the sinister "Men in Black"—weird black-clad men who intimidate UFO experiencers into keeping their mouths shut. For this reason, black helicopters made their way into the writings of the legendary author and investigator John Keel.

President Obama admitted to the existence of mysterious black helicopters in 2015. He said, "There are black helicopters." Of course, he prefaced his statement with: "But we generally don't deploy them on U.S. soil." Mmm hmm. Sure.

For decades, I have heard rumblings of a vast network of secret tunnels that connects various government sites in Washington, D.C., with offsites in Virginia and beyond. Some say there is even a high-speed rail network underground. At minimum, there are subterranean highways connecting these sites, according to believers. These sites include, but certainly are not limited to, Mount Weather in Bluemont, an underground city and centerpiece of the federal government's Continuity of Operations (COOP) plan; Mount Pony in Culpeper, the former site of a Federal Reserve doomsday bunker; Warrenton Training Center; and Raven Rock Mountain Complex in Pennsylvania.

There are other, lesser-known shadowy government facilities scattered throughout the commonwealth. Spears Mountain in Buckingham County and Peters Mountain in Albemarle County come to mind. It seems no one really knows what goes on in these places. Then there are the covert sites operated by various three-letter agencies, oftentimes fake companies used

Impressive stonework on the grounds of Mount Pony. *Courtesy of Nicole Pierce.*

Outwardly, Mount Pony in Culpeper County looks rundown. *Courtesy of Nicole Pierce.*

to hide secret operations. There are countless warehouses, office buildings and industrial park units all over Northern Virginia, the Shenandoah Valley, Richmond and the Tidewater region serving as cover for clandestine government activities. Top-secret programs are literally hiding in plain sight. After all, why do you think there are so many mattress stores, many of which are rarely open and almost empty inside? Newsflash: the average American rarely buys a new mattress—certainly not often enough to support the number of mattress stores per capita.

JOHN WILKES BOOTH GOT AWAY

My favorite conspiracy centered on the commonwealth does not involve mattress stores, secret sites, nefarious government programs or even black helicopters. This conspiracy goes all the way back to April 26, 1865, when Union army sergeant Boston Corbett shot and killed President Lincoln's assassin, John Wilkes Booth, in Port Royal, Virginia. Or at least, that is what the powers that be would have you believe.

John Wilkes Booth was born in Bel Air, Maryland, in 1838. He came from a long line of stage actors and was a popular actor himself. Booth was the "Brad Pitt of his day," according to some, and called the "handsomest man in America" at one point. As the country inched closer to civil war, Booth was firmly committed to the Southern cause. After the Commonwealth of Virginia convicted John Brown of treason and murder for his raid on Harpers Ferry, Booth traveled to Charles Town (now West Virginia) to watch Brown hang. When war broke out between the states, Booth made a vow to his mother that he would not enlist in the Confederate army. However, he came to hate himself for not joining the fight. In a letter to his mother, Booth wrote, "I have begun to deem myself a coward and to despise my own existence."

Booth became determined to fight the Union in another way. In 1864, he devised a plan to kidnap President Lincoln and deliver him to Richmond as a hostage. Booth worked with Confederate spy John Surratt and a team of Confederate sympathizers on the plot. The group routinely met at the boardinghouse of Mary Surratt, John Surratt's mother. But when General Lee surrendered at Appomattox Courthouse, Booth abandoned the kidnapping plan and decided instead to kill Lincoln.

On the night of April 14, 1865, Booth carried out his dastardly deed as Lincoln watched a play at the Ford's Theatre in Washington, D.C. Booth walked up behind Lincoln, shot him in the head and leaped onto the stage. Being true to the actor he was, Booth shouted, "*Sic semper tyrannis*," the Latin phrase and Virginia motto, meaning "thus always to tyrants."

Booth fled Washington and made his way into southern Maryland, where Confederate sympathizers aided him in his escape. Booth crossed the Potomac River and landed in Virginia in King George County near Upper Machodoc Creek. Booth then headed to Bowling Green, where Colonel John Mosby and his troops were camped, and on April 24, he took refuge at the Garrett farm near Port Royal.

During all of this, the Federal army had launched an intense manhunt for Booth and his accomplices. The government offered a $100,000 reward for information leading to the arrest of Booth, the equivalent of about $1,800,000 today. On April 26, Federal soldiers trapped Booth and an accomplice, David E. Herold, in a tobacco barn on the Garrett farm. Herold surrendered; however, Booth remained inside and refused to come out. The soldiers set the barn on fire, and as Booth moved about inside, Sergeant Boston Corbett shot him in the neck. Booth died a few hours later. A military tribunal found Mary Surratt, Lewis Powell, David Herold and

An 1890 photograph of Mary Surratt's boardinghouse at 604 H Street in Northwest Washington, D.C. *Library of Congress.*

George Atzerodt guilty of the conspiracy to kill Lincoln and hanged them on July 7, 1865. The tribunal handed down prison sentences to four other conspirators. Those are the official events. But as my old buddy Brad said, "You can't trust the government, you can't believe the news and the history books are full of crap." So, what really happened?

An artist's interpretation of Lincoln's assassination. *Library of Congress.*

In the early 1870s, a drifter named John St. Helen showed up in Granbury, Texas. He was a mysterious, dark-haired, good-looking man with a hot temper. He worked as a bartender, and most thought he had too much money for his line of work. St. Helen was also a bit too cultured for the Texas frontier; the eloquent speaker often quoted Shakespeare.

In 1872, St. Helen hired attorney Finis L. Bates to handle federal charges against him for selling alcohol and tobacco without a license. St. Helen confided in Bates that he was living under an assumed name, though it was not until years later that he explained why. St. Helen and Bates became friends, and about five years after they met, St. Helen became ill. His sickness worsened until death seemed imminent. Believing he might not make it through the night, St. Helen summoned his friend Bates to his bedside. Through ragged breaths, St. Helen made a shocking confession: "I am dying. My name is John Wilkes Booth, and I am the assassin of President Lincoln. Get the picture of myself from under the pillow. I leave it with you for my future identification. Notify my brother Edwin Booth, of New York City."

Obviously, the confession stunned Bates. But he did not believe St. Helen was really Booth; he could not reconcile the man he knew—his friend—with being a cold-blooded assassin. Bates would get the chance to talk with St. Helen again and receive clarity on the confession. Not only did St. Helen

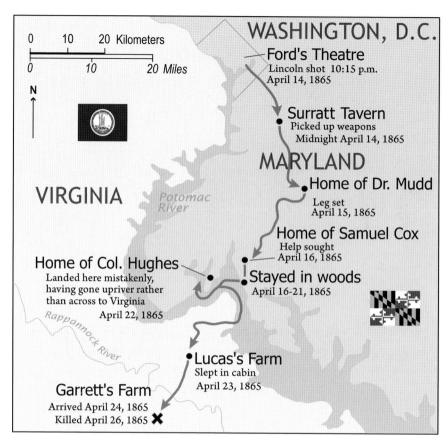

This is the escape route John Wilkes Booth used after he killed President Lincoln. *Wikimedia Commons.*

live through the night, but he went on to make a full recovery. Months later, St. Helen gave a detailed confession to Bates.

According to St. Helen, he had acquired over $20,000 in gold during his acting days. He had deposited this money in various banks, some in Canada. He used this money to finance the Lincoln kidnapping plot and later for his escape after the assassination. St. Helen implicated Vice President Andrew Johnson in the plot and, in fact, claimed that Johnson had urged him to kill Lincoln after Lee surrendered. It was Johnson who told him where Lincoln would be, and it was Johnson who arranged his escape from the city. A network of Confederate sympathizers delivered him to Colonel Mosby at Bowling Green, and from there he made his way to the Garrett farm.

St. Helen told Bates that while he was at the Garrett farm, Confederate supporters warned him when Federal troops had crossed the Rappahannock

The War Department placed a hefty bounty on the head of John Wilkes Booth. *Library of Congress.*

River in pursuit of him. He hid in the woods and was not present when the soldiers surrounded the tobacco barn. The man Boston Corbett killed was named Ruddy—a man he had paid to help him escape. Ruddy had dark hair and a similar build; he also had a check from Booth for sixty dollars, Booth's letters and a picture of Booth. These items, the similar physical appearance

A military tribunal sentenced four of the conspirators in the Lincoln assassination plot to death by hanging, including Mary Surratt. *Library of Congress.*

and a rabid desire to see the president's assassin apprehended led to the misidentification of the dead man.

Having injured his leg during his jump on the stage after shooting Lincoln, St. Helen easily disguised himself as a wounded Confederate soldier and made his way west, relying on the sympathy of folks along the way. He headed through West Virginia and crossed the Big Sandy River into Kentucky. He continued west across the Mississippi River, eventually going as far as the Indian Territory, where he "remained at different places, hiding among the Indians for about eighteen months." He went on to San Francisco, where he met his brother and mother, and then to Mexico before finally settling in Texas under the name John St. Helen.

St. Helen offered his confession to Bates because he wanted to set the record straight. He was troubled that the authorities hanged Mary Surratt; she was innocent and knew nothing of the assassination plot. He hoped his confession would clear her name. He also did not like the newspapers calling him an assassin. St. Helen swore he was not a callous, evil man and he took

Was Vice President Andrew Johnson in on the plot to kill President Abraham Lincoln? *Library of Congress.*

no pleasure in killing Lincoln. He feared that after the Confederacy fell, the Union would mete out harsh punishment against the South and confiscate land and property from its citizens. He believed if Andrew Johnson, a Tennessean, assumed the office of president, the southern states would fare better in the aftermath of the war.

Once the cat was out of the bag and St. Helen had revealed his true identity, he left for Colorado. Bates informed the War Department that Lincoln's killer was still alive, but nothing came of it.

Fast-forward to 1903. Bates had moved to Memphis, Tennessee, and St. Helen's whereabouts were unknown. That is until a man named David E. George died by suicide in Enid, Oklahoma. The *Encyclopedia of Oklahoma History and Culture* says the following:

At approximately 10:30 a.m. on January 13, 1903, in the Grand Avenue Hotel in Enid, the screaming of a guest who had occupied room number four for three or four weeks brought others to his side; David E. George was soon dead. A doctor diagnosed the cause of death as self-administered arsenic poisoning. Later it was told that the deceased had purchased strychnine that morning at a local drug store. The body was taken to Penniman's Furniture Store, also a funeral home. A coroner's jury soon heard stories about this strange, locally unknown man: he was a house painter who did not know how to paint, who always had access to money but died penniless, who frequented bars and loved alcohol, who often quoted Shakespeare, who knew no one but was known by many outside Enid, who was quoted as saying, "I killed the best man that ever lived."

After George was embalmed, he was placed in a chair in the window of the furniture store/funeral home so that the public could view him, and a photograph was taken. It was believed that he had a "remarkable likeness" to Booth and that his leg had been broken above the right ankle—the same break that Booth had suffered in jumping from the Ford's Theater balcony....Just as public interest was beginning to fade, Finis L. Bates from Memphis, Tennessee, arrived in Enid. Bates identified the body as his old friend John St. Helen.

There are other conspiracy theories regarding the escape of John Wilkes Booth. Some believe he escaped and stole the identity of an Englishman named John B. Wilkes and lived out his days in Indiana. Booth's distant relatives had long heard rumors of Booth's escape, handed down through the family for generations, and went to court to have Booth's body exhumed and DNA tested. A judge ruled against the family. But the cover-up does not end there. The man killed in the Garrett barn underwent an autopsy. The coroner removed several vertebrae from the body, and these are on display at the National Museum of Health and Medicine in Washington, D.C. The museum has rejected requests by the Booth family to have DNA extracted from the vertebrae. I wonder why—it almost makes me think the government knows it got the wrong man.

Chapter 17

OLD HOUSE WOODS

Most folklore has a kernel of historic truth.
—Rosalind Hammond

There is a plot of wooded, undeveloped land in Mathews County that, if stories are true, encapsulates everything in this book and more. Located about five miles east of Mathews in the unincorporated community of Diggs lie Old House Woods. This unique place is home to legends of buried treasure, phantom animals, skeletal figures, a flying ghost ship and most anything else you can imagine.

A popular treasure legend that comes from Old House Woods is the tale of the Cornwallis treasure. According to legend, when British general Lord Cornwallis retreated through Virginia on his way to Yorktown, he sent six soldiers to the Diggs area to bury a wagonload of treasure he had collected. The supposed treasure would be worth north of $2,500,000 today. According to *Treasure Legends of Virginia* by Charles A. Mills, "The soldiers buried the treasure but shortly thereafter were killed in a skirmish. The location of the treasure died with them."

The Old House Woods treasure stories go back even further. Long before the American Revolution, King Charles II may have sent treasure to Virginia that ended up in Old House Woods. In *Ghosts of Virginia's Tidewater*, L.B. Taylor wrote:

> *After being defeated at the Battle of Worchester, Charles II of England was said to have considered coming to Virginia. In preparation for his trip,*

a group of followers dispatched several chests of money, plate and jewels to the colony by ship. However, for some unexplained reason, the ship never reached Jamestown. Instead, the ship sailed up the Chesapeake Bay and anchored in waters at the mouth of White's Creek near Old House Woods. There, the treasure was offloaded, but before it could be safely hidden, the Royalists were attacked by and murdered by a gang of indentured servants.

There is no such thing as a clean getaway. Karma always has a way of catching up. In their haste, the indentured servants only grabbed a portion of the loot, planning to come back for the rest later. But tomorrow did not come. The bandits died at sea after their boat sank in a storm.

Some think pirates buried treasure in Old House Woods. One legend states that a group of pirates hid their loot in the woods and shortly thereafter perished in a storm. In another pirate tale, the infamous Blackbeard "intercepted the treasure and then murdered the men who were hiding it." Some think it is these murdered pirates who haunt the fifty-acre tract of pines and marshland. Over the decades, witnesses have spotted apparitions "feverishly digging" in Old House Woods. The specters work by "phantom lantern light." Perhaps this is a replay, or residual energy, from one of these events long ago.

Bernhard Gillam's 1885 illustration of a shipwreck following a *Flying Dutchman* sighting. *Library of Congress.*

Perhaps the most bizarre tales from Old House Woods are the reports of a ship that flies over the Chesapeake Bay. Phantom flying ships have long been a staple of maritime lore. The most famous example is the *Flying Dutchman*, a ship that failed to make it into port and is forced to roam the seas forever. The ship emits an eerie glow and hovers over the water. For centuries, sailors around the globe have spotted the *Flying Dutchman*; seeing the ghost ship is a bad omen.

Of course, skeptics have their answer for the *Flying Dutchman* and other phantom ships. Many point to a phenomenon known as "superior mirage" to explain flying ships. Temperature inversion—when cold air collects near the water with warmer air above it—can bend light, forming an image that makes it look as if a ship is sitting in midair rather than floating on the sea. While this phenomenon probably explains the vast majority of ghost ships, the explanation falls short at Old House Woods. Here, witnesses have seen a ship "hovering over the woods as the men aboard climb down rope ladders toward the ground." Needless to say, a mirage cannot cause that. Maybe these phantom figures climb down into the woods in search of the treasure buried there.

A flying ship is not the only vessel that shows up at Old House Woods—there is also a Spanish galleon that appears in the bay and vanishes into thin air. Phantom cows and horses also make random appearances at Old House Woods. Why? And why do witnesses claim to see armor-clad skeletons carrying swords? Other strange phenomena at Old House Woods include a headless man walking around looking for a lost lover and a "storm woman" who appears above the trees and shrieks to warn sailors of impending danger.

Why is all this weirdness taking place at Old House Woods? I can't help but wonder if there is a doorway or window to another world here. Or are we dealing with a "time vortex"? Science fiction concepts aside, time has stood still at Old House Woods. Rosalind Hammond, a Mathews County native and former dean at Bowling Green University, said, "Old House Woods is unique because it is relatively undisturbed. It's right on the water and has not been developed. It hasn't been contaminated. The channel has long filled in but it's probably one of the places in Mathews that is closest to its original form."

Maybe being "right on the water" is the key to the strangeness at Old House Woods. The aforementioned L.B. Taylor Jr. believed Virginia's Tidewater region is one of the richest areas in the nation for metaphysical activity. He wrote, "Edgar Cayce, arguably the greatest American psychic, believed that because two large bodies of water (the Chesapeake Bay and

A view of Old House Woods from Haven Beach in Mathews County. *Author's collection.*

The author's dogs enjoying a summer day at Haven Beach. *Author's collection.*

the Atlantic Ocean) were involved, the area was particularly conducive to paranormal forces." Additionally, Taylor pointed to the "four hundred years of civilized settlement" in Virginia that led to more "trauma and tragedy" than any other state in the Union. This trauma has created "fertile spawning grounds for spectral phenomena."

But of course, not everyone agrees. There is no shortage of naysayers who claim the stories are nonsense. "I've lived there all my life and never saw anything," is a common refrain. But that is how it goes with these tales, and regardless of the location and its reputation, for every believer there is a skeptic. No amount of eyewitness testimony will convince a skeptic; likewise, debunkers will never deter enthusiastic believers.

I was talking to a fellow who wants to film a documentary at Old House Woods. I told him as far as I knew the land is privately owned. He knew that, but still, he wanted to investigate the legendary place and bring it to the big screen.

"I stayed about thirty minutes from there in the RV," I told him. "Me and the wife and our dogs visited Haven Beach a couple of times. It's right beside Old House Woods. I can tell you those woods look like they'd be creepy as hell at night."

"Oh, I bet," he replied.

"I've read that a lot of locals say most of the stories are BS."

"No way. There has to be something to all those stories."

"I think so, too. Maybe some of it is embellished, but those stories come from somewhere."

"What else are they going to say? Of course they're going to deny it."

"I guess so. Buried treasure, a flying ship, a disappearing ship, a banshee, ghosts digging in the woods, skeletons carrying swords, ghostly animals…I'd probably deny it, too."

SELECT BIBLIOGRAPHY

Books

Bahr, Jeff, Troy Taylor and Loren Coleman. *Weird Virginia: Your Travel Guide to Virginia's Local Legends and Best Kept Secrets.* New York: Sterling Publishing Co. Inc., 2007.

Barden, Thomas E. *Virginia Folk Legends.* Charlottesville: University Press of Virginia, 1991.

Bates, Finis L. *The Escape and Suicide of John Wilkes Booth.* Naperville, IL: J.L. Nichols & Company, 1907.

Bergman, Sandi, and Scott Bergman. *Haunted Richmond: The Shadows of Shockoe.* Charleston, SC: The History Press, 2007.

Coleman, Loren, and Patrick Huyghe. *The Field Guide to Bigfoot and Other Mystery Primates Worldwide.* New York: HarperCollins, 1999.

———. *The Field Guide to Lake Monsters, Sea Serpents and Other Mystery Denizens of the Deep.* New York: Jeremy P. Tarcher/Putnam, 2003.

Cushing, Jonathan P. *Collections of the Virginia Historical and Philosophical Society.* Richmond, VA: Thomas W. White, 1833.

Eberhart, George M. *Mysterious Creatures: A Guide to Cryptozoology.* Santa Barbara, CA: ABC-Clio Inc., 2002.

Fox, Amaryllis. *Life Undercover: Coming of Age in the CIA.* New York: Alfred A. Knopf, 2019.

Godfrey, Linda S. *Hunting the American Werewolf: Beast Men in Wisconsin and Beyond.* Madison, WI: Trails Books, 2006.

Green, John. *Sasquatch: The Apes Among Us.* Blaine, WA: Hancock House Publishers, 2006.

Hall, Marie Bauer. *Foundations Unearthed.* Los Angeles: Veritat Foundation, 1974.

Haywood, Mike. *Tales My Father Told Me: Ghosts, Treasures & Legends of the Virginia Peninsula & Beyond.* N.p.: self-published, 2021.

Hunter, John P. *Witches and Ghosts, Pirates and Thieves, Murder and Mayhem: Scary Tales from Colonial Williamsburg.* Williamsburg, VA: Colonial Williamsburg Foundation, 2007.

Kinney, Pamela K. *Haunted Richmond, Virginia.* Atglen, PA: Schiffer Publishing, Limited, 2007.

———. *Virginia's Haunted Historic Triangle: Williamsburg, Yorktown, Jamestown & Other Haunted Locations.* Atglen, PA: Schiffer Publishing, Limited, 2019.

Lindsey, Hal, and Carole C. Carlson. *The Late Great Planet Earth.* Grand Rapids, MI: Zondervan, 1970.

Mills, Charles A. *Treasure Legends of Virginia.* N.p.: self-published, 1984.

———. *Urban Legends of Virginia.* N.p.: self-published, 2015.

Mosby, John S. *The Memoirs of Colonel John S. Mosby.* Boston: Little, Brown and Company, 1917.

Pulitzer, Jovan Hutton. *10 Treasure Legends! Virginia: Lost Gold, Hidden Hoards and Fantastic Fortunes.* N.p.: self-published, 2014.

Schlosser, S.E. *Spooky Virginia: Tales of Hauntings, Strange Happenings, and other Local Lore.* Guilford, CT: Globe Pequot Press, 2010.

Taylor, L.B., Jr. *Ghosts of Virginia's Tidewater.* Charleston, SC: The History Press, 2011.

———. *Haunted Virginia: Ghosts and Strange Phenomena of the Old Dominion.* Mechanicsburg, PA: Stackpole Books, 2009.

———. *Monsters of Virginia: Mysterious Creatures in the Old Dominion.* Mechanicsburg, PA: Stackpole Books, 2012.

Virginia Beach Public Library. *The Beach: A History of Virginia Beach, Virginia.* Virginia Beach: Virginia Beach Public Library, 1976.

Williams, Lloyd Haynes. *Pirates of Colonial Virginia.* Richmond, VA: Dietz Press, 1937.

Articles

Arment, Chad. "Virginia Devil Monkey Reports." *North American BioFortean Review* 2, no. 1 (2000).

Baker, Donald P. "In VA., a Battle over Buried Treasure." *Washington Post*, July 7, 1998.

Boston News-Letter. "The Death of Blackbeard." February 23, 1719.

Boyd, Bentley. "Mystery Vault May Yield Papers of Francis Bacon." *Baltimore Sun*, August 21, 1992.

Bulletin (Philadelphia, PA). "Chesapeake 'Monster' Filmed." July 12, 1982.

Calvert Marine Museum. "Chesapeake 'Chessie,' Myth or Monster." *Bugeye Times* 4, no. 1 (1979).

Campbell, Beverly. "When Virginia Ducked Milady Witch." *Richmond Times-Dispatch*, December 30, 1934.

Clayton, Cindy, and Jack Dorsey. "Mysterious Boom, Tremors Rattle Folks All Over Area." *Virginian-Pilot*, June 10, 1997.

Collins, Denis. "Chessie and His Ilk: De-Monsterably Shy." *Washington Post*, December 9, 1984.

———. "The Creature from Dismal Swamp." *Washington Post*, July 12, 1981.

Daily Morning Journal and Courier (New Haven, CT). "Monsters from Dismal Swamp." March 11, 1902.

Davis, Richard Beale. "The Devil in Virginia in the Seventeenth Century." *Virginia Magazine of History and Biography* 65, no. 2 (1957).

Gilliss, Chas J. "A Buried Treasure." *Fairfax County Historical Society Yearbook* 3 (1954).

Goochland Gazette. "Could Goochland's 'Devil Monkey' Mystery Be Solved?" July 17, 2014.

Gup, Ted. "Underground Government." *Washington Post*, May 31, 1992.

Harden, Blaine. "The Mount Vernon Monster." *Washington Post*, May 12, 1979.

Lyons, Richard. "Chessie Sightings Are a Monster of a Claim." *St. Petersburg Times*, October 21, 1978.

Mussulman, Joseph A. "Soundscapes: The Sonic Dimensions of the Lewis and Clark Expedition," *We Proceeded On* 21, no. 4 (1995).

New York Times. March 11, 1863.

———. "Details of the Evacuation." April 8, 1865.

Rappahannock Record (Kilmarnock, VA). "Treasure Hunter Says There's Gold along Beaches." May 22, 1986.

Richmond Dispatch. "The Dismal Swamp 'Monster.'" February 18, 1902.

Rouse, Park. "Pirates Left Evidence but No Treasure." *Daily Press* (Newport News, VA), May 17, 1992.

Rural Retreat Times. "Dismal Swamp Monster." April 18, 1902.

Spartanburg Herald. "Chessie Is Back in the Potomac." June 26, 1980.

Sunday Times (Salisbury, MD). "Marines Have 'Big Foot' of Their Own." February 6, 1977.

Times (Richmond, VA). "The Dismal Swamp Monster." April 13, 1902.

Virginia Department of Historic Resources. "Historic Architectural Survey of Cumberland County, Virginia." October 17, 1994.

Washington Post. "Are There Fortunes to Be Made If We Just Knew Where to Look?" October 5, 1984.

———. "Man in Bunny Suit Sought in Fairfax." October 22, 1970.

———. "The Rabbit Reappears." October 31, 1970.

Websites

BBC News. "Double-Nosed Dog Not to Be Sniffed At." August 10, 2007. news.bbc.co.uk.

Bigfoot Field Researchers Organization. "Geographic Database of Bigfoot/ Sasquatch Reports & Sightings." www.bfro.net.

Conley, Brian A. "The Bunny Man Unmasked: The Real Life Origins of an Urban Legend." Fairfax County Public Library. www.research. fairfaxcounty.gov.

Costantino, Grace. "The Beautiful Monster: Mermaids." Biodiversity Heritage Library. blog.biodiversitylibrary.org.

Cox, Jeremy. "Mystery of Chincoteague's Loud Boom Deepens." *Delmarva Now*, September 24, 2015. www.delmarvanow.com.

Davis, Robert. "Confederate Gold." New Georgia Encyclopedia, March 26, 2020. www.georgiaencyclopedia.org.

Dutton, Nick, and Wayne Covil. "Mysterious Booms Baffle Central Virginia Residents." WTVR CBS 6, January 7, 2014. www.wtvr.com.

Forbes, Timothy C. "The Clifton Bunny Man." Castle of Spirits. www. castleofspirits.com.

Gardner, Chris. "Chasing Chessie." *Bay Weekly* 22, no. 45. November 6, 2014. bayweekly.com/chasing-chessie.

Gomez, Kelly. "Virginia Ghost Town Abandoned by the Railroad." The Forgotten South. theforgottensouth.com.

Holmberg, Mark. "The Legend of the Ghost Light of Cohoke, West Point." WTVR CBS 6, October 25, 2014. www.wtvr.com.

Hubbard, Francis. "The Legend of Old House Woods: Professor to Share Research on Spooky Mathews Site." *Daily Press*, April 19, 2016. www.dailypress.com.

Keeton, Louise. "Paranormal Investigators Tell the Tales of Virginia's Ghosts, Werewolves, and Vampires." VPM, September 30, 2021. vpm.org.

Kilar, Steve, and Timothy B. Wheeler. "Chessie the Manatee Pays Return Visit to Chesapeake Bay." *Baltimore Sun*, July 15, 2011. www.baltimoresun.com.

Kollatz, Harry, Jr. "W.W. Pool: Richmond's Reputed Nosferatu." *Richmond Magazine*, October 30, 2013. richmondmagazine.com.

Larsson, Anna M.K. "Dogman/Werewolf Sightings Map." The Cloaked Hedgehog. thecloakedhedgehog.wordpress.com/the-map.

Logsdon, Guy. "Booth Legend." *The Encyclopedia of Oklahoma History and Culture*. www.okhistory.org.

National Security Agency. "The Beale Papers." www.nsa.gov.

National UFO Reporting Center. "National UFO Reporting Center Report Index by State/Province." www.nuforc.org.

NBC 4 Washington. "Spooky Creature Creeping Around Va. Neighborhood." October 19, 2011. www.nbcwashington.com.

Neal, Emily. Goochland County Devil Monkey Official Sightings Blog. goochlanddevilmonkey.wordpress.com.

Paullin, Charles. "NASA: Friday's Loud Boom in Shenandoah County Was a Fireball." *Northern Virginia Daily*, September 21, 2021. www.nvdaily.com.

Philips, Douglas, and Barnaby Nygren. "An Inquiry into the Validity of the Legend of Braddock's Gold in Northern Virginia." Fairfax County Historical Society. www.fairfaxhistoricalsociety.org.

Schwartzman, Paul. "Bigfoot Discovered? Virginia Man Says He's on Verge of Bigfoot Discovery." *Christian Science Monitor*, June 7, 2010. www.csmonitor.com.

Scribner, Vaughn. "Fabricating History: The Curious Case of John Smith, a Green-Haired Mermaid, and Alexandre Dumas." The Junto, June 16, 2015. earlyamericanists.com.

Strickler, Lon. Phantoms and Monsters. phantomsandmonsters.com.

University of Virginia. "The Countryside Transformed: The Railroad and the Eastern Shore of Virginia, 1870–1935." eshore.iath.virginia.edu/node/2095.

Vela, Hatzel. "UFO Sighting in Loudoun County?" WJLA ABC 7, January 3, 2014. wjla.com.

Virginia Chapter of the North American Dogman Project. "Sightings in Virginia." www.vadogmanresearch.com.

Virginia Ghosts. "Update on the Richmond Vampire." September 29, 2001. web.archive.org/web/20010929154332/http://www.virginiaghosts.com/vampire_update.htm.

Virginia Tourism Corporation. "Virginia Is for Lovers." www.virginia.org.

Warwick, S.E. "More on the Goochland 'Devil Monkey.'" Goochland On My Mind, December 15, 2010. goochlandomm.blogspot.com.

Washington Post. "Mystery Boom Rattles Parts of Va." May 11, 2011. www.washingtonpost.com.

WTVR CBS 6. "Loud Booms Came from Fort Pickett Live-Fire Training, Officials Say." February 27, 2022. www.wtvr.com.

ABOUT THE AUTHOR

The author at McAfee Knob in Catawba, Virginia. *Author's collection.*

Denver Michaels is an author with a passion for cryptozoology, the paranormal, lost civilizations and ancient history and all things unexplained. The Virginia native has written over ten books examining unexplained phenomena, including *Haunted Shenandoah Valley*, *Giants: Men of Renown* and *Strange Tales from Virginia's Mountains*.

Michaels and his wife travel the country full time in an RV with their beagle. He is an avid outdoorsman and, in his spare time, enjoys sightseeing, investigating the unexplained and working on future books.

Visit us at
www.historypress.com